Sannyasa

Cultivating Spiritual Awareness

With kind regards, ॐ and prem

Sannyasa

Cultivating Spiritual Awareness

Swami Niranjanananda Saraswati

*Discourses from the Yogadrishti (Yogavision) series
of satsangs at Ganga Darshan Vishwa Yogapeeth,
Munger, from 2nd to 6th January 2011*

Yoga Publications Trust, Munger, Bihar, India

Published by Yoga Publications Trust
    First edition 2011

ISBN: 978-81-86336-95-3

Publisher and distributor: Yoga Publications Trust, Ganga Darshan, Munger, Bihar, India.

Website: www.biharyoga.net
         www.rikhiapeeth.net

Printed at Aegean Offset Printers, Greater Noida

Dedication

*To our guru Sri Swami Satyananda Saraswati
who continues to inspire and guide us
on our spiritual journey.*

Contents

1

Ideal of Sannyasa

On 5th December 2009, our guru, Sri Swami Satyananda Saraswati, attained mahasamadhi. We had just concluded the Yoga Poornima celebrations on 2nd December. During that event he said that he was still waiting for his 'return ticket' and that he would not go till it was granted to him. Then, three days later, he called up Swami Satsangi at 10.30 in the night and said, "I have received my return ticket and I am going to go today." On being asked when, he said, "Now."

By the time Swami Satsangi reached his place of residence, she found him seated in meditation. At a certain moment he folded his hands and prayed, "God, I am ready to come, take me." He drank a few sips of Ganga water, placed tulsi leaves in his mouth, went deeper into meditation, and left his body with the chanting of *Om*.

Even when Sri Swamiji left his body, he taught us a lesson. He gave us a lesson on how to die in a yogic manner, as for him death was as much a celebration as life. Before he brought up his pranas and left the body, he made a specific sound through his mouth, a sound which is customarily made during marriage in Bengal and also in some aboriginal tribes. The tongue is struck against the upper palate again and again very fast and the sound that emerges is ulu-ulu-ulu. The custom is therefore called performing 'ulu' in Bengal. It is an indication that union of two people is taking place. Sri Swamiji made this sound indicating that union of his soul with the Supreme Soul was taking place, and left his body.

We read about yogis, rishis and siddhas renouncing their pranas at will. Until now one had only heard about this, one had not seen anyone do it. Sri Swamiji proved that what is written on the leaves of history is true; it is possible. Of course it was not a difficult feat for him, for he was an unusual person.

Fibre of a sannyasin

Sri Swamiji was a true sannyasin and his whole life exemplifies sannyasa. One must understand that the process of sannyasa and a sannyasin are two different things. When you look at Sri Swamiji, you see in him what you want to see. You want to see him as guru, so you see him as guru. You haven't seen him as a sannyasin, so you do not know his sannyasa aspirations and the trials that he had to go through as a sannyasin.

In sannyasa one has to go through a process of education, not initiation. Most aspirants go through the process of initiation and not education. The process of education is primary in order to become a sannyasin and initiation is secondary. However, for most aspirants initiation becomes primary and they are not interested in education.

Just because you have shaved your head and been initiated with a name, mantra and colour does not mean that you have become a sannyasin. If you think you are a sannyasin, think again. Think whether you are living the life of a sannyasin. Don't be a donkey in the skin of a lion. By wearing the skin of a lion the donkey does not become a lion. For most aspirants who come to the path of sannyasa and take sannyasa, it is like putting on the covering of a lion, but their heart remains that of a donkey, their speech remains that of a donkey, their expectations and desires remain that of a donkey. They don't become the desires, expectations, strength, force, confidence or character of a lion. Therefore, remember that initiation into sannyasa and being a sannyasin are two different things. There is a sloka:

Aabaddhakritrimasataajatilaamsabhitti
Raaropito mrigapateh padavim yadi shvaa
Mattebhakumbhatatapaatanalampatasya
Naadam karishyati katham harinaadhipasya.

If one ties a lion's mane around the shoulders of a dog
and seats him on the throne of the king of beasts, can
he roar like the fierce lion that dashes out the brains of
a mighty, mad elephant with a single stroke of his paw?

There have been very few people in history who have been
the lions of sannyasa, who have been able to uphold the
highest standards of sannyasa and also take the tradition
forward. Swami Sivananda was one of them and Swami
Satyananda was another. They presented the lifestyle and
lifelong sadhana of a sannyasin by living it.

There are many who take sannyasa, but there are very few
who live the real life of a sannyasin. Anybody can be initiated
into sannyasa; every Tom, Dick and Harry has the right to

3

take sannyasa, of course, if they qualify. These days sannyasa has also become a business; people think that if they take sannyasa they will be recognized as gurus. They will acquire disciples, make ashrams, and live in luxury on the earnings of disciples. It is true that many people think in this way. People want to create institutions, have disciples, and earn name and fame. However, a sannyasin does not have any desires for himself; in fact, he does not have any desires in life. One who lives as a sannyasin is a person with a different character, a different mentality, a different perception and a different attitude in life. Such people become the examples of a *parampara*, tradition. And this is what we find in the gurus of our tradition: both Swami Sivananda and Swami Satyananda lived as sannyasins.

Medium of grace
There is a story. Once there was an aspirant who performed intense *tapasya*, austerities, for many years. His goal was to have the *darshan*, vision, of God.

God was pleased with his tapasya and appeared before him. Now, whenever God travels down to earth it is for only one reason: some human has asked him for something. People keep praying, "God, give me this. God, do that for me." Therefore, it has become God's habit to say, "Ask for a boon!" the instant He manifests before a human. So when He appeared before this aspirant also the first thing He said was, "Ask for a boon!"

The aspirant replied, "God, it is your grace that I have been granted your vision. The only purpose of my sadhana was to receive your darshan and that has been accomplished. So thank you very much, now you may go back to your heavenly abode." God said, "I cannot leave without granting you something." The aspirant replied, "I am not a businessperson who practises give and take." God insisted, "But now that I have come here, you have to ask for something." The aspirant replied, "Aren't you omnipresent and omniscient, don't you reside in everyone's heart?" God

4

replied, "Yes." The aspirant said, "Don't you know what is in every being's heart?" God replied, "Yes." The aspirant said, "Then how come you don't know what is in my heart?" God said, "What do you mean?" The aspirant said, "There is no desire in my heart. If you call yourself omniscient, then you must know that there is no desire in my heart; the only desire was to have your darshan and that has been fulfilled."

God said, "Yes, I do know, but what can I do! Every time I come to samsara, the software of my mind changes into the giving mode and the words 'Ask for a boon!' come out of my mouth automatically. The beings of samsara have worked on my mind in such a way that I must play this role whenever I come here. It was by mistake that I spoke those words, O aspirant, and I ask for your forgiveness. However, as the words have been uttered, ask for something. My word will then be honoured."

The aspirant said, "No, I don't want anything," and turned his back and walked away. He thought, "If I continue to stand here having God's darshan, God will continue to harass me. It is better that I leave, and when He finds that I have gone He will also leave." With these thoughts, he prostrated before God, performed namaskara, turned his back and left. God was totally perplexed. He thought, "My devotee is walking away without taking anything from me! But I have given my word and I must give him something. Yet, if I attempt to do so I will displease him. What should I do?"

As God watched the aspirant leave and wondered what to do, suddenly He noticed the man's shadow. It was sunset time, the aspirant was walking towards the sun and his long shadow was reaching up to God. God thought, "Wonderful! Found the solution! I will not bless the aspirant, I will bless his shadow. May whoever it falls upon become happy, healthy and prosperous."

The aspirant did not know that his shadow had received this boon. He kept on walking, and wherever his shadow fell miracles took place. It fell on a sick person and he was cured. It fell on a blind man and he gained eyesight. It fell on a lame man and he could walk. It fell on a dying tree and it became green and laden with flowers and fruits. In this way, without the aspirant's knowledge, his shadow continued to perform miracles. The shadow became the medium of God's grace.

This is what happens to true sannyasins. Our param-guru, Swami Sivananda, and our guru, Swami Satyananda, were such kind of bhaktas. They never desired anything for themselves. At the age of sixty-five Sri Swamiji left Munger, an age at which every individual is only concerned about se-curing the future. After establishing such a large institution and initiating a yogic revolution he left everything to walk his path alone. Only a person who is not influenced by his karmas can do this, and such a person is a sannyasin.

For a worldly person attainments are everything, while for a non-attached person renunciation is the cause of at-tainment, and attainments are the cause of bondage. You feel happy in attainments, but a sannyasin feels bound in attain-ments. Expectations rise and desires become sky-high when there are attainments. And who do you go to when you are not able to fulfil your intense desires? You go to a sadhu or a siddha, unload your sack of desires and problems on him, and ask for a solution so you can be free of their weight and bondage. So, for a sannyasin attainments are bondage and renunciation is freedom.

Today, when we observe Sri Swamiji's life, we find that it always exemplified the qualities of a sannyasin and that was also his teaching to us.

Inherent connection with higher self

A sannyasin is one who remains established in the higher self, and the ability to connect with his spiritual psyche was always a very strong trait in Sri Swamiji. Even when he was very young, at the age of six, he would frequently become unconscious. People would think that he was having an epi-leptic fit or that for some reason his blood pressure tended to fall suddenly. However, doctors would find nothing wrong with him. It was the sannyasins and sadhus passing through the village who would say, "This is not an illness, this child is endowed with special qualities. He is a yogi. His state of unconsciousness is not akin to fainting, it is a state of samadhi. He achieves samadhi spontaneously; it is not savikalpa or nirvikalpa, it is not nirbija or sabija, but sahaja, completely natural." But of course a child of six cannot fathom, understand or comprehend a state of samadhi, nor can society. What it indicates is the type of samskara he came with, which allowed him to have that level of experience when he was only a small boy.

Implicit faith in guru

Sri Swamiji's spiritual samskaras led him to his guru, Swami Sivananda. The guru recognized the diamond and polished it. Swami Sivananda did not teach him yoga. Sri Swamiji tells in his own words, "I never went to any class, whether of hatha yoga, philosophy or anything at all." Swami Sivananda told him, "Work hard and the light will shine."

This statement is an indication that one needs to first clean oneself, become empty, remove the dross, the impressions of

gross, material life, recondition oneself, adopt new thoughts, live new qualities and a new awareness. Once one is able to do that, then the journey in spiritual life will begin. Thus, Sri Swamiji immersed himself in hard work, with no time to participate in the classes on yoga, vedanta, philosophies or religions, no time to pursue any spiritual practice.

Swami Sivananda knew that although spiritual awareness is the birthright of everyone, to come to that point there has to be a lot of preparation. There has to be a lot of understanding, adjustment and awareness. Therefore, he always said, first clean the building in which you are going to live. This was the idea which Swami Sivananda infused in his disciples, not in the yoga practitioners or visitors, but in those who were willing and determined to live in the house that was given to them, but only after having cleaned it.

With implicit faith in the statement of his guru, Sri Swamiji worked hard. He followed the instructions of Swami Sivananda to the letter. If I tell anybody, "Work hard," they will say, "But when can I do my yoga nidra? When do I get to do my asana and pranayama?" Sri Swamiji did not ask this of his guru.

Most disciples are *manamukhi*, mind-oriented, not *gurumukhi*, guru-oriented. They are controlled by their desires, passions, anger and disturbances, and that is why they don't progress. The first duty of a disciple is to be gurumukhi, not manamukhi and not *samsaramukhi*, world-oriented. However, 99.9 percent of disciples are samsaramukhi and manamukhi, only 0.1 percent are gurumukhi. If a guru can find even one such disciple, his mission becomes successful. Ramakrishna Paramahamsa found one – Swami Vivekananda. He had many disciples, but only one Swami Vivekananda won over the world. Swami Sivananda found many such disciples, for such was God's will, and they triumphed all over the world. And Swami Satyananda said, "I am giving you two flowers . . ."

A disciple who is gurumukhi will forget all the problems and pains of life and only think of how to fulfil the guru's orders. This is what we see in the life of our guru. Till the last moment his thoughts were connected with his guru. Till the very end he perceived himself as a disciple. I believe that when Sri Swamiji went into mahasamadhi, Swami Sivananda must have stood before him and Sri Swamiji would have had his darshan, for the relationship between guru and disciple is very intimate, very deep. It is a relationship of the spirit.

There comes a time in the graph of a disciple's evolution when he has to become gurumukhi. Being samsaramukhi makes one see duality, but discipleship matures when one does not look at the world, but only at the guru. This is what Sri Swamijji practised, and people such as him become the architects of a culture. Society does not create culture; society does not bestow strength to a civilization. The creator of a culture is the sannyasin or the spiritually awakened person; it is they who provide stability on a civilization. A sannyasin always remains established in the higher consciousness, in his guru. This is a state of life in which the *sankalpa shakti*, power of resolve, becomes very intense, and that is what awakens discipleship.

Exceptional talents
One born to be a true sannyasin will also display exceptional talents. Sri Swamiji was gifted with a photographic memory. In the days when he lived with his guru there were no tape recorders or computers. Perhaps the first generation Remington typewriter had been recently invented. There were no pens, only pencils, and even the paper was not fine like now but the rough type. Sri Swamiji would listen to Swami Sivananda's lectures and satsangs for an hour or two hours, then he would sit before the typewriter and type out the entire lecture word by word, including breaks and stops. The next morning he would present it to Swami Sivananda. The satsangs were held in the evening, he would type it out at night, and in the morning at four o'clock he would present the ready manuscript to Swami Sivananda. The work done by a recording machine today, Sri Swamiji could do through

his mind. For this is a mental talent; it is a speciality of the mind, it is an indication of an awakened mind.

Swami Vivekananda was also gifted with an exceptional memory. You may have heard the story of how he would take books from a library, read the contents by just turning the pages and the next morning return them. The librarian did not believe that he could have read so many books in such a short time, so when she questioned Swami Vivekananda on the contents, he could repeat the words from the books verbatim. This was due to a photographic memory. In the same way, Sri Swamiji would listen to a satsang and type it out word for word. In this way, his mind, feelings and actions remained connected with his guru's words, teachings, behaviour and actions.

Ordinary people have great difficulty in imbibing anything. If they listen to a satsang or lecture and you ask them, "Which teaching could you remember? At least repeat one teaching that you have remembered and imbibed from the satsang," they reply, "There were so many nice things that I've forgotten everything. You said so many things, it was amazing." And in their amazement they forget it all. However, Sri Swamiji would write down everything he heard and that was how it was possible to propagate Swami Sivananda's teachings at that time. Due to this, Swami Sivananda also awarded him the title of 'Jnana-Yajnopabhrit'.

Becoming guru's instrument

It was through the satsangs, through this interaction and proximity that Swami Sivananda was able to bring forth the *vidya*, knowledge, from within Sri Swamiji.

When he told Sri Swamiji, "Now go out and propagate yoga," Sri Swamiji said, "But I don't know yoga. You are asking me to do something that I don't know at all." Swami Sivananda took him to his room and in fifteen minutes initiated him into kriya yoga. It was not the kriya yoga which you practise, not vipareeta karani mudra, anuloma viloma, Om and so on. When Sri Swamiji uses the words kriya yoga, he is

10

referring to the transmission of knowledge that took place in those fifteen minutes between Swami Sivananda and Swami Satyananda. Transfer of information from one hard drive to another hard drive. The connection which brought these two hard drives together was implicit understanding, total faith and trust between guru and disciple.

Guru's eulogy to an able disciple

Swami Sivananda has praised Sri Swamiji in unequivocal terms. Nowhere in recorded history has a guru spoken on the qualities of his disciple in this way. Disciples speak about their gurus, but for a guru to speak about the qualities of a disciple is extremely rare.

Swami Sivananda described Swami Satyananda as someone who is full of Nachiketa qualities. The Nachiketa quality is an absolutely selfless quality. It is the quality of discrimination, stability, fearlessness. It is the quality which

makes one free from attractions and repulsions. It indicates a person who is not even afraid of death.

Swami Sivananda's words are the eulogy of a guru to his disciple. What more can a guru say about his disciple? It indicates what kind of a disciple or person Swami Sivananda perceived Sri Swamiji to be. Endowed as he was with all these qualities, one can also imagine what kind of a perception, association and feeling Sri Swamiji had for his guru. It also goes to prove that Sri Swamiji was gifted with special samskaras and that he was born on this earth for a special purpose.

A sannyasin's method of revolution

When Swami Sivananda told Sri Swamiji, "Go and propagate yoga," he did not come out and tell people, "I've been ordered by my guru to open an ashram and teach yoga, so please help me." He said to himself, "My guru has given me an order. I will fulfil it, but I will find a way by which this system can reach each and every person in society." With this thought in mind, he travelled for nine years without establishing a centre or ashram. For nine years he simply observed what the need of human society was and how yoga could help people overcome their difficulties. He contemplated on how yoga should be presented, whether as a spiritual science or a practical science, what the form and method of presentation ought to be. It was after nine years of analysis and contemplation that he started the ashram in Munger, and came to lead the yogic renaissance all over the world.

Such clarity and perception is not ordinary. Such understanding and planning is not ordinary. Place yourself in that situation, what would you have done? Only a person who is completely dedicated to his guru follows such a course of action. He thinks, "I have been given an order by my guru, therefore I will execute it to the best of my ability." Such a person does not go by the whims of his mind; he will not teach whatever occurs to him. He takes into consideration what people need, and only such a person can bring about a revolution. Only a person who is free of ambitions, who is completely surrendered and has absolute faith and trust in guru or the higher reality can be a visionary. He is able to see not only the immediate consequences, but also the distant future, and accordingly establish a program.

Perfecting six stages of sannyasa

In the tradition it is stated that a sannyasin goes through six levels of education and experience in order to reach the pinnacle of sannyasa. Looking at Sri Swamiji's life from this perspective, he too followed this sequence and achieved perfection in each stage.

Kutichak: When an aspirant first experiences the desire to transform his state of mind, he lives in the guru's ashram as a novice. At this stage he is known as kutichak, and for twelve years he is required to live as a kutichak.

Kutichak means one who lives in a *kutiya* or hut. In the olden days the ashrams used to consist of huts, so it refers to a person who lives in the guru's ashram. When Sri Swamiji lived in Rishikesh at his guru's ashram he lived as a kutichak, serving his guru, imbibing and learning from the proximity of guru, until the light within shone brilliantly and Swami Sivananda said he was ready to go out in the world. Sri Swamiji had lived in the guru's ashram for twelve years and now the guru sent him out with the mandate, 'Spread yoga from door to door and shore to shore'.

Bahudak: The second stage of sannyasa is bahudak. This is where the sannyasin moves in society to spread the teachings of the guru after receiving and imbibing them. *Bahudak* means one who moves with many or interacts with many. When Swami Sivananda sent Sri Swamiji out and, following his guru's mandate, he travelled and worked to propagate yoga, recognized the needs of society and worked to fulfil the mandate of his guru, he was in the stage of bahudak.

Hamsa: The third stage is that of *hamsa*, which means swan. It refers to a person who becomes stable in one place and can also move about. He can move about in society and come back to his place. When Sri Swamiji came to Munger and established the ashram, became firm in his place and started to teach yoga, his stage was that of a hamsa.

Paramahamsa: In the fourth stage of *paramahamsa*, supreme swan, the sannyasin attains the pinnacle of his inner evolution and aspires for the welfare of many.

When Sri Swamiji renounced what he had created, when he detached himself from his own creation, he settled in the state of paramahamsa. Now, even his own creation had no attraction for him, he was free from it, free from the attachment, the need and influence of power, people and prosperity, from name and fame. He renounced everything in an instant. The moment he renounced everything that he had helped create as a dedication to his guru, he had fulfilled the mandate of his guru. There were no other desires left, and he became established as a paramahamsa.

Trigunateeta: In the fifth stage, the sannyasin becomes free of every law of society and remains established in the higher consciousness. This is the stage of total inner renunciation. When Sri Swamiji established himself in the higher consciousness through his sadhanas he became *trigunateeta*, one who is beyond the three gunas.

Avadhoota: In the sixth stage the sannyasin becomes an avadhoota, one who is free of all limitations of nature. *Avadhoota* means one whose garb is space. He is one who has totally discarded all worldly ties and represents the pinnacle of spiritual evolution. For him nothing is righteous or unrighteous, holy or unholy. He is free of karma. The karmas of this life and past lives are all burnt away, and due to the absence of *kartritva*, doership, and *bhoktritva*, desire for enjoyment, no future karmas are created.

Constant effort

The six stages in the life of a sannyasin have been prescribed by the tradition; however, not many are able to live up to them. Many aspirants come to the stage of kutichak and stop their journey there. Many remain as bahudak and stop their sannyasa journey there. Very few come up to the stage of hamsa and paramahamsa.

Even as a sannyasin, continuous effort has to be made to pass one class and move to the next, on and on. Sannyasa is not a static state. In the life of our guru, I see this progression. He has lived the tradition, he has been victorious in struggles, the austerities, and come out with flying colours, winning and smiling because of his selflessness.

Sri Swamiji was always a paramahamsa. In Rikhia he exemplified the states of trigunateeta and avadhoota. His consciousness, his heart, his actions were harmonized with these states, and so was everything that happened around him. It was not necessary for someone like him to perform such hard austerities like the panchagni, for he had already attained everything. However, he did it so that others could learn and be inspired, and so that a tradition could be established. These sadhanas have been performed in the past only by rishis and munis in vedic times. It is the first time in modern history that a sannyasin has performed them. Likewise, Swami Sivananda also performed intense sadhanas. Therefore, they are the luminaries of sannyasa. Only people such as them are known as sannyasins according to our tradition.

Epitome of sannyasa

The quality which makes Swami Satyananda a true sannyasin is, in fact, the Nachiketa quality. Living at the pinnacle of selflessness. Not starting the journey towards selflessness, but living at the pinnacle of selflessness. That is the highest quality of a sannyasin.

Selflessness is something that must be expressed in a practical way, not in a theoretical way. You do not say, "I have become selfless." Those who become selfless don't have to say it. If you say "I am selfless," you are identifying with your ego, so how could you be selfless? You are with the self, you cannot be selfless. So, don't think that selflessness is easy to acquire; it is the most difficult thing in the world. You can give things away in charity, but that is not selflessness.

Selflessness means the state where one's thoughts are never about oneself. In Sri Swamiji's life I have never seen him think about himself, not even once. In all my years of association with him I have never seen him think about himself. To come to this state of a sannyasa, one has to pass through a modification of the normal self, and Sri Swamiji's life shows us how to do it.

2

Origins of Sannyasa Tradition

Sannyasa is a very ancient tradition of India with its founda-
tions in remote history. As communities, villages and towns
were being developed by the agrarian society thousands of
years ago, some people left the comfort, security and safety
that the community provided them with, and lived in isolation. They began to think and reflect about the purpose,
aspirations and goal of human life: why do we come here and
where do we go from here. They were the people from whom
the tradition of sannyasa originated.

Rishis and munis

The thinkers were called munis. A *muni* is a person who reflects and thinks. The munis gave birth to different schools of
thought which came to be recognized as philosophies over a
period of time. These trains of thought or philosophies covered
every subject that an individual lives and experiences in the
course of a lifetime. They were the authors of the Vedas and
Puranas and their ideas gave clear indications of an individual's
relationship and association with society, the world, nature and
divinity. Apart from providing ideas and thoughts to adopt in
life, they also offered a sequence of disciplines which could
enable people to discover what the sages themselves were experiencing and talking about in their philosophies.

Out of this group, there were those who focused on
prolonged and intense practice of the methods they had

17

developed and experimented with. They attained higher states of consciousness and were able to perceive the future, past and present. They could assess the needs of the community and provide direction to them through their example and teachings. They were the rishis or seers. *Rishi* means a person who has the ability to see far, a visionary.

In this way, a community of people developed who had left the society, but who were thinking about further development of society in an integrated way. They were thinking of how people could provide a purpose to their life and beautify it. The munis and rishis were the original renunciates from whom the sannyasa tradition started. Although they lived in isolation, their effort was aimed at beautifying the community. In isolation they perfected themselves, attained the highest state of consciousness and became realized, but they came to the community and shared with others what they had gained.

The rishis and munis followed their path, system, aspiration and vision in every way they could. They lived a life of hard discipline but high spiritual attainments. Emulating them, many others from society came forward to experiment and adopt a different way of life. At this stage they were often called *tyagis*, renunciates, people who had wilfully left society to follow a particular path which was not the main stream of social living and conditioning.

Even today the path society supports is that of economics and technology, all that is physical and material. Society does not support spiritual learning. Which school anywhere in the world teaches spiritual science? There may be centres that you visit due to your personal inclination, but spiritual organizations are not supported, aided, encouraged or developed by governments as a national activity. The situation was the same in the past. So these people left wilfully, knowing that they were leaving behind the social and material opportunities in order to pursue a different train of thought. They went to the isolated dwelling places of the rishis and munis, and lived there as sadhus, virtuous, pious people.

Sadhu means a good or pious person, one whose slate is clean. It is a broad term used to refer to all categories of renunciates. Once the sadhus had the right environment to pursue their aspirations, they began to practise austerities, sadhanas and tapasyas. They started exploring and experimenting and in the process systematized yoga, tantra and other views and thoughts. All these different schools of knowledge and experimentation were clubbed together in one category, *adhyatma vidya* or *paravidya*, spiritual science or transcendental knowledge.

Development of gurukuls and ashrams

Eventually the rishis became the educators of society, and around them sprang up gurukuls or communities where people could be educated in both social and spiritual sciences. That was the beginning of a gurukul.

The learning in a gurukul was imparted by a guru: a capable, enlightened and knowledgeable person who headed the gurukul. People from every walk of life, from both prosperous families and deprived families, would come to learn there. Along with social sciences, they would learn spiritual disciplines. They would also be made to face hardships so they might become physically, mentally, emotionally and spiritually strong. Whether they were princes or children of the poor they would all have to sleep on the hard floor, cut wood and gather fruits and berries from the forest. The gurukuls were centres of hard discipline and hard work. They were places where one would receive both positive *samskaras*, impressions, and *shiksha*, education.

Traditionally, a twelve-year period was set aside for gurukul education and in this period, sixty-four *kalas* or arts were taught. Art means an expression of life, whether intellectual or creative. Any form of expression in life is an art. At the gurukul this could include study, mantra, japa, dhyana, asana, pranayama and so on. Ashrams were originally gurukuls, centres of learning where social as well as spiritual disciplines could be imbibed, where skills to survive and excel in the material world and to explore one's inner potential were both taught.

In recent times the concept of gurukul has changed in India. Generations ago, when invaders came into this country, they brought their own ideas of education and systems of life and overpowered the local traditions and customs. The gurukuls were now split into two. The institutes that taught social sciences were called schools, colleges and universities, and the places where spiritual science could be learnt were called ashrams, maths and peeths. An ashram is a public community which is open to everyone, a math is a closed community and a peeth is the source of teaching. This is how gurukuls were later categorized. Society took on the responsibility of shiksha or education and left the responsibility of providing samskaras to ashrams. Therefore, while the role of schools, colleges and universities is to teach how to live in society, the role of ashrams is to provide the methods to harness one's inner potential. They teach the methods to harness, balance and use the energies of the mind properly in order to achieve excellence.

This is how the ashrams must be understood even today. Ashrams are not yoga centres, religious centres, spiritual clubs or spiritual communities. An ashram is a place where one can cultivate the right samskaras that help one live in a better way on retirement from active social life. However, such a role can be played only by an ashram which upholds a tradition, has continuity of inspiration and a vision. An ashram cannot be equated with a school, college or university. The whole approach here is self-observation and fine-tuning of the individual nature and personality.

Social education and spiritual education both fulfil a role in life. However, today we have forgotten the purpose of education. We think that education only improves an individual's status in society. We think that if one is educated, one will have more opportunities and options to achieve better heights in life. However, that view is only social, for such education has utility only as long as one is active in society. When one becomes inactive in society, the utility of spiritual education becomes evident, for spiritual education brings forth human creativity. Social education sharpens one's intellectual capacity, but spiritual education engages one's intellectual, emotional as well as spiritual potential. Therefore, it brings about a more comprehensive and integrated development.

In the future, social education and spiritual education will have to come together again. They will have to come together if there is to be peace in life. Right now with only one type of education in society, there is no peace or contentment in life, there is only competitiveness. Soon, an integration of these two systems will again take place and the different stages of life can then be lived with an understanding of the relationship between human nature and divinity. That will make human life complete.

Shankaracharya's role

Now, while the tradition of recluses who developed the spiritual sciences and philosophies of India is very ancient, sannyasa as an order was provided a defined structure in the eighth century by Shankaracharya. This was a period in history when the purity of the vedic tradition was becoming corrupted and rigid ritualism had taken over. Buddhism had emerged as a counterforce and was becoming increasingly popular. The genuine keyholders of vedic wisdom no longer moved among the masses, but remained isolated and dispersed. At this time a young man called Shankaracharya came forward as a mighty force and sought to restore the vedic tradition.

Shankaracharya was a very gifted person. At the age of eight he took sannyasa, which means that he was a born sannyasin. There were no karmas or samskaras to guide him in the ways of the material world; right from the beginning he was directed to the path of spirituality. He was a genius who brought together all the renunciates, recluses, tapasvis, sadhakas and aspirants under one banner. That banner of

sannyasa was not a religious banner; it was the banner of a philosophy known as Advaita Vedanta.

Beyond duality: By tradition every sannyasin is a Vedantin, an adherent of Advaita Vedanta, which is not a religion but a liveable philosophy. Sannyasins do not form part of any cult, religion or system, but come under the banner of Advaita Vedanta.

The philosophy of Advaita Vedanta says: discover the highest self within and you will know that you and the higher self are not two different expressions. However, before you discover the higher self, *paramatma*, cultivate knowledge, awareness and understanding of the pulls, attractions and deceptions of *maya*, illusion, and keep yourself free from them. When you are able to remain free from the deceptions of maya, you will realize paramatma. And once you realize paramatma, you and your Father are one.

Western scholars of the past did not understand this system of thought; they clubbed together everything spiritual in India under one heading, Hinduism, as they were familiar with the concept of religion which existed in their society. They were not familiar with the concept of spiritual awareness or spiritual consciousness and they said, "All these constitute part of Hinduism, and Hinduism is a religion." Since then people have associated the word 'Hinduism' with a religious group, conditioning, belief, lifestyle, motivation and aspiration. However, if you as a seeker look into the tradition, religion plays no role in the life of a sannyasin.

Under the banner of Vedanta, many different schools of thought have converged. When one becomes a sannyasin, one renounces the religion that one had identified with earlier. One is now above religion.

The biography of Ramakrishna Paramahamsa mentions that he lived like a Muslim for some time. For this period he followed all the practices of a devout Muslim. He practised the daily prayers and followed the strict discipline of Islam. For some time he lived like a Christian, a strict Catholic, following all the rules and laws of Catholicism. In this way,

Ramakrishna Paramahamsa lived different religions, cultures and traditions.

A religious-minded person would never do anything like this. They would never let go of their belief system. Only a sannyasin would. In the life of Sri Swamiji we have seen that he has lived everything. We have seen him conduct Christian Mass, Islamic prayers, Sikh path; he has practised everything. Would you call Swami Satyananda a Christian? Would you call him a Muslim? Would you call him Hindu? What would you call him? I would call him a sannyasin. A sannyasin who has a clear understanding of the process that leads one to experience the highest qualities within. And the highest qualities within are *Satyam*, *Shivam* and *Sundaram*, beauty, truth and auspiciousness.

If you come to that level, there is no concept of duality any more. Everything is Satyam, Shivam and Sundaram. That is Advaita Vedanta: no difference. Difference is a creation of the mind, a creation of one's character or nature. When this character, nature or mind dissolves, then where is the difference? There is no difference any more.

Shankaracharya's philosophy of Advaita Vedanta states that all rivers meet and merge in the ocean, and in doing so they lose their individual identity. In the same way, all thoughts and beliefs merge into the supreme reality; they do not maintain separate identities when they reach there. At the end, the entire creation and all individuals merge into the supreme spirit, and that supreme spirit exists in all, even though it is formless, nameless, unmanifest and unimaginable.

Acceptance of form: Despite his adherence to the non-dual philosophy, Shankaracharya admitted that to reach that beginingless, unmanifest entity, one needs the help of a manifest element. He himself worshipped forms and established customs of worship. He was a believer in the formless God and the tenet of non-duality, which held that there is only one truth in creation; the individual is under the deception of *maya*, illusion, and the world of illusion

24

is transitory. However, he also upheld the wisdom of form worship.

While it is true that eternal life is only to be found in the indestructible reality, to reach it one needs a rope, just as one needs a rope to fetch water from a well. Even if you get close to the formless reality, you cannot attain it unless you have a bucket and a rope. A bucket is able to hold the water of the well; it limits the water into a container so you can make use of it. In the same way, the form is the limited manifestation of the formless. That which you can identify is the form and that which is expansive is formless. This is a theory of physics and it is also a spiritual principle.

After all, how did life evolve? It started with a single-cell organism, an amoeba. It expanded and assumed the forms that we recognize now. Slowly it transformed and we received this body made up of the five elements. The unmanifest formless reality is like that cell. It is a seed which contains the potential for both creation and destruction. A seed is formless, you cannot see the tree in it. However, that formless power sprouts and turns into a plant and then a tree. When that force assumes a form you see the trunk, the leaves, the flowers. Therefore, the form is the method or stepping stone to reach the formless. Shankaracharya accepted this and thus bhakti and worship find a place in Advaita Vedanta.

Dashnami tradition: Sri Adi Shankaracharya gathered all the sannyasins and structured the tradition of renunciates. When Shankaracharya reorganized the tradition of sannyasa, he divided the sannyasins into ten categories based on the places where they were living. This tradition still exists and is known as the dashnami tradition. *Dashnami* means ten kinds of names. For instance, if I lived beside the seashore, I would receive the epithet 'Sagar': Swami Niranjanananda Sagar, indicating the place where I stay, for *sagar* means sea. If I lived in a city, then I would be called Swami Niranjanananda Puri. If I was a forest dweller, I would be called Swami Niranjanananda Aranya. If I was a jungle dweller, I would be called Swami Niranjanananda Vanam. In this way, the dashnami order came into existence, and provided strength to the tradition.

When thousands of thinkers, wise people, sages and saints come under one banner, a culture and a civilization receive immense strength. Therefore, these sannyasins, living in their own locations throughout the country, became a major force to bring about a cultural and spiritual transformation. It was these sannyasins who developed and sustained the spiritual culture of India. They worked selflessly and brought about a philosophical revolution in society. They brought about a revolution in the samskaras of society so that people became aware of their inherent spiritual duty, their dharma. The word *dharma* does not mean religion. It has been defined as: *Dharayate iti dharmah* – "The positive quality that you are able to hold is dharma." The positive thoughts, actions and behaviour that you express is dharma. However, we have associated dharma with *aradhana* or worship. Today the term dharma is used in the context of ritual practice. If I say, "Think in the right way," you would not consider it dharma. The definition of dharma has changed. Shankaracharya's efforts brought people to the path of dharma in the original sense of the word, so that society was re-injected with the right samskaras. Till recently dharmic samskaras predominated in the social structure of India. It is only in the last one or two generations that materialism has gained strength and the new generation that is emerging is equipped with education, but not samskaras.

Establishment of maths: Shankaracharya also established four monastic institutions called maths at four different corners of the country, with the idea that the spiritual heritage should spread uniformly throughout the land. These were: Sharada Math in Dwarka, Sringeri Math in Sringeri, Jyotir Math in Badrinath and Govardhan Math in Puri. Through the maths he was able to unify the various and diverse groups of sannyasins which were scattered throughout the country and bring them all under the one banner of vedic dharma. The maths were founded as the headquarters for the

26

sannyasins of different traditions and the heads of the four maths became the direct representatives of Shankaracharya. They were also meant to help the *parivrajaka* or wandering sannyasins. The four maths still exist as the nuclei of the sannyasa tradition in India and their heads are still called Shankaracharyas.

3

Ashrama System

Purpose and Path

Thousands of years ago, our ancestors contemplated the evolution, development and growth of human life, and arrived at a conclusion. They said that every individual must live an integrated and balanced life from birth to death. In order to live such a life they defined four stages of life that one must pass through, and these stages were called ashramas.

The word *ashrama* means a place of hard work. By ashram people generally think of a spiritual community; however, ashram means a place where one comes to work. *Shram* means effort, labour or activity; therefore, ashrama means the place where one performs a specific activity. A *yogashrama* means a place where yoga activity is being conducted; it does not mean a yoga community or yoga centre. In the same way, *sannyasashrama* means a place where the activities of sannyasa are being conducted. So, the entire spectrum of life is divided into four ashramas: four areas, compartments or divisions, each of which represents a specific kind of activity that one must focus on in that stage.

Four stages of life

In the first stage of life one equips oneself with knowledge and wisdom of the world to survive in the world. In the second stage of life, with the knowledge, wisdom and under-

28

standing that one has acquired, one works to support one's family, society, nation and world. In the third stage of life, when one has handed over the charge of one's responsibilities to the next generation, one spends time in reflection, contemplation and the discovery of one's self. In the fourth stage, after one has established oneself in contemplation and personal discovery, one goes out to help and uplift those in need so they can overcome their physical, mental, spiritual, social and psychological difficulties.

The first two ashramas or chapters of life are called *brahmacharya* ashrama and *grihastha* ashrama: the stages of learning and taking on responsibilities. The other two are *vanaprastha* ashrama, the stage of acquiring wisdom, and *sannyasa* ashrama, the stage of surrendering oneself to the higher will. In the first half of life one equips oneself and satisfies one's whims, desires and needs, and tries to propagate a good culture in the family and society. Here, one's involvement, participation and education are in relation to the material world, the world of senses and sense objects. In the second part of life, one re-educates oneself, not only for self-development but with the awareness that one can help uplift others too. The second part deals with developing spiritual awareness, which is the destiny of every human being.

This is the way of life prescribed by the ancients. However, somewhere over the passage of time, the appropriate understanding was lost. People became involved in the pleasures of the senses and the belief that life is only meant for the first two stages, brahmacharya ashrama and grihastha ashrama. That became the mould for society to emulate, and for hundreds of years this is how people in society have lived, despite having an understanding that life is not complete if one stops at grihastha ashrama.

The spiritual masters and traditions, however, have maintained the principle of the ashramas even now, and exemplify that the second two stages of life should also be lived in order to complete the journey.

Purpose of brahmacharya and grihastha ashramas

The first stage of life, brahmacharya ashrama, is the learning stage. When we are young, we go through a process of education; we learn and equip ourselves with the tools and knowledge to survive in society and be recognized in society. That is the novice state in which we receive the skills of survival. This process of education is external; it is oriented towards society, profession and money.

The learning received in the brahmacharya stage becomes the base of life. The education and samskaras that one receives at this stage, the mentality and perspective that one forms, the understanding that one acquires, become the base of life. After receiving these skills for survival, the individual moves into another dimension, area or compartment of life, grihastha ashrama, where social and family responsibilities are taken up.

In grihastha ashrama, one makes the effort to fulfil one's obligations and commitments to family and society and offer the best of one's endeavours to them, and at the same time to fulfil one's own aspirations, needs and desires. Propagating a family, entering into a profession, acquiring a job, enhancing one's wealth, acquiring name, fame and status, post and power, all these constitute part of the grihastha stage. It is the medium and means to acquire and fulfil all one's ambitions and desires.

Our ancestors said that in the first part of life where one is living one's learning and responsibilities, one is able to fulfil two roles: *artha*, material security, and *kama*, desire. The learning is intended to acquire material security; whether you become a doctor, engineer or geologist, it is for the fulfilment of your artha. Your involvement in family and society, and the constant effort to improve the quality of your material life represent your kama. A better car, better clothes, better food, better comforts, better luxuries, the latest gadgets: these are the fulfilment of kama. Thus, one lives artha and kama during brahmacharya ashrama and grihastha ashrama. However, this is not a permanent state. A break comes naturally when

30

the new generation becomes ready and takes up duties and responsibilities. They come forward and you take the back seat.

Vanaprastha: moving into the spiritual dimension

When one takes the back seat, one embarks on 'the retired life'. This is when the third compartment of life is entered into. The baton of responsibilities and duties has been handed over to the next generation and one enters into a life of reflection, contemplation, study and development of personal creativity, and acquiring a deeper understanding of human nature so that one can help others. This is vanaprastha ashrama. One has retired from active service in

life and is becoming a passive witness to the world while the new generation takes up its roles.

Usually when people retire, they still spend their time pursuing material pleasures. In the West they go travelling. They say, "I have worked hard all my life, now I am going to see the world." They buy a round-the-world ticket, hang their cameras around their necks, wear floral shirts and shorts, and travel the world. When they return home, they show their pictures to everyone; "Look, I was in Abu Dhabi, I was in Rome, I was in Munger, I was in Rikhia." That is the life of a retired person in the West. In India they want to stay with their children and solve their problems, believing they are still indispensable. Those who can afford may go travelling or on pilgrimages.

Now, I would ask all retired people: what has been your achievement in life since you retired? When you were active in your profession you could define your achievements in terms of your promotions, acquisition of wealth and objects of desire, but what are the parameters of your achievement upon retirement? When your profession does not define your identity, then what was and what should be your duty and responsibility?

Our ancestors said that when one becomes free from social responsibilities, one must focus on the cultivation of dharma in life. In the social system of ancient India, when the new generation came forward, the head of the family would hand over all responsibilities and no longer stay with them. Even kings would give up the kingdom to the heir and retire in seclusion to lead a life of contemplation. The tradition held that once the worldly responsibilities are handed over, one is free of all obligations and debts, whether of society, family, friends or parents, and therefore one may prepare for the next stage of life. This is when one needs to pack one's bags for the next journey. Of course it takes time to pack one's bags, but how many of you have even started? Have you even opened the suitcase? Instead, you spend your time regretting what you have not done when you find that the body is becoming weak and the memory dim.

32

There is no attempt to cultivate spiritual awareness at any stage in the life of an average person. They may visit their church, temples or other places of worship, but a personal spiritual life does not exist for them; a sadhana, a spiritual discipline or spiritual awareness does not exist for them. People simply follow the path that many others before them have taken.

Spiritual life has to be cultivated. Sri Swamiji says that the purpose of human life is to cultivate spiritual awareness. He does not say that the purpose of human life is to have self-realization. He says the purpose of human life is to cultivate spiritual awareness. How high you take it is your effort and sadhana. You can go as high as you want, but keep on with the effort of cultivating spiritual awareness. This effort is the focus of the second two compartments of life.

Paths of pravritti and nivritti

There is another thought in spiritual life offered by the sages. There are two paths of life: one takes you towards the material world while the other takes you towards the spiritual world. The first is called the *pravritti* path, which means entering the maze of vrittis. *Vrittis* are modifications, behaviours or patterns of mind. These behaviours, patterns and modifications of mind are like a maze. You can enter into a maze, but finding the way out is next to impossible. So, the pravritti marga means going in the direction of the material world, the senses and sense objects, into the maze created by the sense objects and losing your bearings in it. The other path is the *nivritti* path where these patterns, conditions and behaviours of mind which suck you in don't exist. You are out of the maze; therefore, there is no pull, sway or attraction of any vritti.

Now these two words, pravritti and nivritti – into the maze and out of the maze – have to be correlated with the first two and latter two life conditions. In the *Bhagavad Gita*, Sri Krishna has spoken about the identification of the mind with sense objects (2:62–63):

33

Sangaat sanjaayate kamah kaamaatkrodhobhijaayate.

From attachment desire is born; from desire anger arises.

Krodhaatbhavati sammohah sammohaatsmritivibhramah.

From anger comes delusion; from delusion loss of memory.

Smritibhranshaad buddhinaasho buddhinaashaatpra-nashyati.

From loss of memory comes the destruction of discrimination; from the destruction of discrimination he perishes.

This is the statement in the *Bhagavad Gita,* reflecting the association of the individual with the world of sense objects. If you look at this statement in relation to your own life, you will discover that it is very appropriate. You have gone through similar states and conditions. You have had conflicts and crises, have gone into depression or anxiety, expressed abnormal behaviour such as being aggressive and vocal, or some other change has taken place in your life due to association and identification with unfulfilled desires, ambitions and expectations.

Lessening of desires indicates growth of the mind. An aspirant once asked Buddha, "What are the milestones of progress in spiritual life? How does one know that one is progressing and advancing in spiritual life?" Buddha replied, "When your cravings lessen, when your desires reduce, when the sensual attractions cause you no grief, then you should know that you are becoming established in spiritual life." Lessening of desires and ambitions, no elation in success and no grief in failure, but maintaining an equipoised mind under all circumstances is an indication of spiritual advancement. This reduction of desires and mental agitation is the path of nivritti. It is the path where the vrittis lessen and one is able to come out of the maze of the mind. The moment you come out from the maze of the mind and become free, you connect with the spirit. And then, the fourth stage of life takes over.

Sockets of material and spiritual life

Materialistic philosophy maintains that enjoyment is the purpose of life, whereas in spiritual philosophy it is said that acquisition of perfection, *poornata*, is the purpose of life. Materialistic philosophy says that acquisition of happiness and satisfaction through material gain is the purpose of life, while spiritual philosophy says that perfection and completeness is the purpose of life.

Many people believe that these two ideas can blend together. People have also made the effort to do so. Each one of you is making the effort to do so. But is it really possible to blend the two? After all, white is white and black is black. When God created day and night, He thought that day was very bright and night was very dark. He said to Himself, "Maybe I should try to blend them together." He tried, and created dusk. He could not mix and match the totality of day and night together, because they are two opposite conditions: presence of light and absence of light. In the absence of light

35

there cannot be any light, and in the presence of light there is only light, so how does one mix presence and absence together? It is not possible. You can have either one or the other. God made the effort and dusk was created. Unfortunately, dusk lasts for a very short time. Even God was not able to blend right and wrong, day and night, positive and negative together. He tried and achieved a very short-lived result. You are trying to do the same thing.

You are trying to blend the material with the spiritual. You want to have your cake and eat it too. You want to be successful here and there at the same time. You want to enjoy the best of both worlds. But is that possible? I have no knowledge of any person who has blended materialistic and spiritual philosophy. Many people experiment and try, but nobody succeeds because these are opposite conditions of life.

Material and spiritual life are like two sockets on the wall. There is one plug, which is you. The plug is connected to one socket and it has three points: positive, negative and neutral; tamasic, rajasic and sattwic. It is continuously receiving electricity from the socket it is connected to, and that is the socket of the material or *annamaya* dimension. The socket beside it is the *anandamaya* or spiritual dimension. How can that plug be connected to the anandamaya socket while it is connected to the annamaya socket? How can it be plugged in to the material dimension and the spiritual dimension at the same time? It cannot be.

You have to pull the plug out of the first socket and insert it in the second socket. When you remove the plug from the first socket, a disconnection takes place. That disconnection is known as *tyaga*, renunciation. It is not external renunciation; it is more a perceptional renunciation: how you identify yourself in the world. If you perceive yourself to be part of the material world, then you can change your thinking and perceive yourself to be part of the spiritual world. It is a perceptional change, perceptional renunciation.

The more you identify with the spiritual, the more frivolous the material will seem. And for those who identify with

36

the material completely, the spiritual is frivolous. This tussle goes on. So the thinkers said, "If you are living the material life, live it fully and just follow certain principles which can make you aware of your higher self internally. In that manner, you can have an awareness and an experience, a glimpse of your own higher nature." They said that by cultivating a certain type of mentality through continuous effort, or *sadhana*, while living material life, one can develop spiritual consciousness. However, you can only go so far, you can go maybe ten percent in the spiritual dimension, for ninety percent of the pull will be from the material dimension. If there is to be a blend at all, it will be only ten or twenty percent. It will enable you to become a good, happy and pious person, to become a good Samaritan.

Now, some people asked, "What if material life doesn't interest us? What can we do then? We just want to pursue the cultivation of our spiritual awareness. We don't want to have anything to do with the outer material world, we want to renounce it." To them the ancients said, "First you have to change your lifestyle. Change your lifestyle, your mind, your attitude, your behaviour, your actions and performance completely. Continue to live in the world, but not with the same mentality, samskaras, attitude or qualities. Try to cultivate better, virtuous and positive qualities. Explore the inherent potential within yourself and allow it to flower." This idea and thought became the foundation of the spiritual journey which begins in vanaprastha: diverting the mind from material objects to the inner self.

When you stop looking at the world and begin to look inwards, that is the beginning of vanaprastha ashrama. When you stop associating and relating with the world outside and begin to develop the faith, confidence, trust and ability to stand on your own feet, that is also vanaprastha. When you are not dependent on the world, on your kith and kin, family and society to survive, then vanaprastha begins.

Vanaprastha also begins when a person has fulfilled all their external commitments. The meaning of vanaprastha is change of lifestyle, change in the direction one has been walking until now. In the past people did go to the forest during this stage to live a life of contemplation, sadhana and swadhyaya. Gradually they developed a system by which in the latter half of life, when one has fulfilled all the external social responsibilities, one can begin to explore oneself.

De-programming the mind in vanaprastha

Our ancestors believed that one has to de-program oneself completely from the input of the senses and sense pleasures, from the input of objects and sense objects in the stage of vanaprastha. One has to re-program one's mind, nature, behaviour, character; one has to re-educate oneself.

The education which you acquired in school, college and university helped you become something in life: a carpenter, an electrician, a doctor, a businessperson or chairperson of an industry. That education shaped the mind in a particular way to enable you to deal with the responsibilities of a profession. By the time you progress through life and come to the pinnacle of success and family life, you condition yourself, your nature and mind by the education you received and the experiences you gained. However, those experiences are useful only as long as you are active in your society, family and profession. When you forego those responsibilities and enter vanaprastha ashrama, you have to first start the process of clearing your mind of the old impressions and re-educating it. You have to clear the mind of the material impressions and re-educate it to understand the deepest inner self.

So, what is the meaning of vanaprastha which allows one to move into this level of experience, this level of reforming oneself? The word vanaprastha means 'one who goes to the forest'. Does this mean that one leaves human society and goes to live in isolation and solitude in the jungle? Does it mean that one struggles to find roots, berries and fruits to eat and wraps tree bark around the body to protect it from cold, rain and heat? No.

Sri Swamiji says that isolating yourself in a cave in the mountains or floating on a boat in the middle of the ocean will not enable you to leave the world. For the world exists in your mind. Therefore, remember that there is no peace in the mountains and there is no noise in the market. The silence and the noise are inside you. If you have an equipoised mind, you will experience peace in the middle of the busiest marketplace and if your mind is disturbed, you will not experience peace in the deepest cave of the Himalayas. These are the words of our guru and today one can understand their validity. Therefore, the word vanaprastha indicates changing the direction of the mind.

Right now your mind is focused in the world, family, friends, name, fame, status, comforts, needs, ambitions, luxuries and all other desires. These desires have to be fulfilled in the material world. However, gradually you begin to identify your actual needs and the perceived needs that you can do without. If you really delve into the details of your life, you will find that the majority of things you hold on to are useless. There is only a sentiment associated with things, which is impractical. Yet, one

39

identifies with those things and doesn't let go of them, whether they be an object, thought, idea or aspiration.

It seems that the thoughts which one develops in childhood, through education, remain right till the end of the day. Thus there is a conflict between this software, which is materially oriented, and the vague aspirations to explore the spiritual realm. Whenever one moves towards the spiritual dimension, the attraction and pull of the senses bring one back to the material reality. Therefore, it is necessary to first change the basic software of the mind. The software one used during the time of learning and education, profession and involvement in society is outdated and not appropriate for the next two stages of life.

In order to change the software, it is the mind that one has to first deal with. Not lifestyle, but the mind. For it is the mind which lives the way it wants to. It is the mind which desires, wants gratification and compels you to follow the desire. It is the mind which identifies with the senses. The input of the senses inspires the mind to associate with objects which give it pleasure. It is due to the mind and its desires that people do not want to go beyond the first two stages of life. They want to remain in class two till the end of their life; no one wants to pass it and move on to the third. It is due to the mind and its desire for enjoyment that they have not been able to connect with the thoughts and actions of dharma and moksha, and believe the phenomenal world to be the only reality. So, it is the programming of the mind which needs to be changed.

Gross and subtle mind

The mind has to be seen in two forms: the material, gross mind and the subtle mind. The gross mind has a particular role and function, and the subtle mind has its particular role and function.

The gross mind is being sustained by the outer experiences. The connection of the gross mind to the world of objects is through the sense organs. It connects with the world, fulfils its desires and enjoys through the medium of the five senses. So, the form of the gross mind is achieved by fusion of the mind with the sense organs.

The gross and externalized mind is searching only for pleasure. Everything that is fed to the mind through the agency of the senses is analyzed from the perspective of its usefulness. The mind asks: "Is this useful to me, does it give me happiness?" If it does, then you attach yourself to that particular object, person or circumstance. If it does not, then there is no personal interest. Thus the gross mind interacts with the sense objects, enjoys them and tries to find pleasure through them. When it does not find pleasure in one object, it moves on to another, then another, and so on.

When one abides in the experience of the gross mind, desire becomes the predominant aspect of life; the same desire rises in the mind again and again, and the mind is continuously pulled towards desire fulfilment. That becomes the nature of the mind. When desire fulfilment and enjoyment becomes the nature of the mind, it becomes *tamasic*, a state in which energy and consciousness both become inert. There is no growth, evolution or movement. There is stagnancy due to which the ego becomes fixed and gets hurt at the smallest pretext.

When desire becomes an inherent part of the mind it is called *vasana*. A desire may be fulfilled, but a vasana can never be satiated. This is the reason why there is so much suffering and discontent at the individual level as well as in society. Unfulfilled vasanas make one fall in the trap of maya, and once trapped by maya it is very difficult to be free. One has to try very hard, come back again and again to work through the vasanas, transform innumerable karmas and samskaras to ultimately become free of the influence of maya.

The gross mind is used in the first two stages of life, as the focus and purpose of the mind in these stages of life is to experience the material world through the senses and fulfil personal desires and aspirations. You are so overpowered by the gross mind that you are not able to think beyond the first

41

two attainments of life, artha and kama. You may be curious about dharma and moksha, but your priority lies in artha and kama. This preoccupation makes the mind conditioned, just as if you draw a picture on a blackboard with a piece of white chalk it will remain there till you erase it. The material world draws a picture on the blackboard of your mind and you want to enter the spiritual world without erasing it. How can you write anything on a blackboard which is already full of writing? You need to first clean it. This is called de-programming. The old karmas and samskaras have to go from the blackboard, so that you can write something new.

Cultivating spiritual life

How can one cultivate spiritual life? The ancients said by fulfilling the roles of dharma and moksha in the second half of life. You fulfil the need for artha and kama in the first half of life and in the other two stages, the focus is on dharma and moksha. These efforts or *purusharthas* have been indicated for every individual.

Dharma is virtuous living, virtuous thinking, virtuous behaviour and in-depth understanding of a situation, of cause and effect. Is this virtuous education a school subject? No. Dharma is not lessons in morality, ethics or virtue. Dharma is appropriate lifestyle, living conditions or manner of living. In the third stage of life, irrespective of the kind of life you have lived till now, try to inject the element of dharma in it. Inject it with positive thoughts, positive behaviour, share the experience and wisdom that you have gained, educate your mind in such a way that the influence of the material world lessens and that of the spiritual enhances. There needs to be a lessening of maya and an enhancement of yoga. The supreme reality has two forms: yoga, which unites, and maya, which separates. In the first half of life the journey is through maya and in the second half it is through yoga, and to accomplish this the efforts of dharma and moksha are advised.

How can one cultivate dharma? After all, everyone knows what is good, right and positive, yet they do not walk that

42

path. There is a very apt statement that Duryodhana makes in the epic *Mahabharata*: *Jaanaami dharmam na cha me pravrittih* – "I know what is dharma, but I am not inclined towards it"; *Jaanaami adharmam na cha me nivrittih* – "I know what is not dharma, but I cannot free myself of it." Therefore, in order to cultivate and understand dharma, to change the software of the mind, the ancestors have defined simple disciplines and rules which allow one to regulate one's life patterns better, develop a better understanding of oneself and one's environment and interactions.

People don't seem to understand or realize the value of discipline in life. They see it as restrictive behaviour. Discipline is not restrictive behaviour. After all, if you ride a horse and the horse says, "You are restricting my behaviour", you will say, "Yes, I need to restrict you if I want to control you. I need to restrict you if I want you to gallop, trot and canter. I may not ride safely if I leave you free."

You tell the guru, "Oh, this method is too difficult", but the guru says, "It is important to hold the reins, without which

43

the rider is totally unsafe." That is one reason why there is so much strife in the world. The riders who are riding the horses of the mind ride unsafely and crash. And remember, you are riding not one horse, but four horses simultaneously.

When I first came to the ashram, Sri Swamiji used to teach me the philosophies of yoga in story form. One day, he told me a story.

A king had four wild horses which were totally untrained. Nobody in the whole kingdom could tame or train the horses. The king made a proclamation, "Anybody who is able to tame and train my wild horses will receive half the kingdom."

Many people came out of greed for the reward. When the horses were brought to them, they tried to ride them the moment they saw them. Of course the untamed and untrained horses gave the riders good kicks and many had broken bones. One day, a young man came to the king and said, "Give me the opportunity. I will try to train the horses, but on one condition. I will take them away with me for one year and return them to you when the year is over." The king agreed. Months passed, the year also passed, fifteen months went by, and the king thought the young man must be dead by now. The horses must have kicked him to death and run away to the forest. He gave up any hope of seeing the horses again.

At the beginning of the sixteenth month, one day the king was strolling on the palace terrace and saw the young man astride a horse and leading the other three. The king met him and said, "You took your time!" The man said, "Yes, I told you one year, but it took me longer. However, I have brought back your horses." The king asked, "How did you train them when so many failed?"

The man said, "I made friends with them. When they ran I too would run, when they walked I too would walk, when they drank water I would make my tea and drink it, when they ate grass I used to make my roti and daal and eat it. Eventually they started to see me as the fifth horse, a bit deformed but nevertheless I was the fifth horse and they accepted me as part of the family. Then, one day, I touched the back of one horse. It jumped, but after a few weeks they became used to my touch. Then one day I put a blanket on the back of a horse. They didn't like it, but after some time they became used to it. One day I put the bridle on a horse, they didn't like it at all, but they got used to it. Gradually, by becoming friends with them, I trained them and today I am able to ride them."

After telling the story, Sri Swamji asked me, "Do you know the names of the four horses?" I replied, "Manas, buddhi, chitta and ahamkara." If I got the answer right he would say, "Ten out of ten." That is how I learnt yoga, through stories. We are not riding one horse, but four horses simultaneously: manas, buddhi, chitta and ahamkara, the four faculties of the mind. It is hard enough trying to train and ride one, but everybody in their zeal and determination wants to ride four horses together. That makes it difficult for both the rider and the horse.

Attaining luminosity of mind

The way to discipline the mind and change the mental software begins with *swadhyaya*, self-awareness, self-understanding, self-analysis, self-observation. The second method is *satsang*, better communication, better understanding, acquiring of wisdom, learning the practical way to apply what one knows in life. The third is *seva*, coming out of the selfish nature and connecting with the selfless nature, observing one's responses and reactions in work. It is easy for people to say, "You have the right to work but you do not have the right to expect results." Can you actually experience that? Can you express that in your life? It is difficult. Through seva, an effort is made to come out of the self-oriented nature, and move towards selfless performance. The fourth method is *sadhana*, improving the quality of the mind by disciplining and regulating it. The fifth is *sanyam* or restraint, which also represents sensorial, psychological regulation.

If one is able to go through this whole process sequentially and systematically with faith and clarity, then the nature of the mind begins to change. It connects with the inner self. The aspiration for pleasure and happiness, which was directing your awareness and attention outwards, now takes you towards the discovery of your true nature. Sadhana brings out the positive quality in you. When the mind is re-conditioned, when the old samskaras and karmas are erased from the blackboard and you are able to write new sentences on it, then the same mind which was connected with pleasure and enjoyment now connects with the spirit. When the material and gross stagnancy of the mind is removed, it connects with the spirit, and then the bondage of maya, of sense objects, break one by one. When this happens, the inherent potential of the mind manifests.

One of the secrets of the mind is that as it becomes freer from the bondage of the senses, desires and expectations, it becomes luminous. It does not cease to exist, instead it becomes more effulgent. The connection with the world represents one's tamasic association. Your interaction and involvement with the world is tamasic, filled with expectations and the desire for self-gratification. On the other side, when the mind is looking inwards, the nature is not tamasic; rather, it is *sattwic*, luminous.

Imagine that there is a powerful lamp, of 10,000 watts. When you turn it on, it is very luminous, so luminous that your eyes cannot adjust to the light. To reduce the intensity of that luminosity, you put a thin covering over the bulb. It reduces the luminosity by, say, five or ten percent. If you want to reduce the luminosity further, you put another piece of fabric over it. You can put as many layers as you want. The more layers you put, the more the light is being confined within the coverings.

The same thing has happened with the mind. The essential nature of the mind is luminous, but the obsessive desires, expectations and ambitions give many layers of covering to the luminosity of the mind. In fact, there are so many coverings that there is no light filtering through and on this side it is all dim and dark. Due to this darkness, you cannot see the road and confusion prevails. In that state of confusion you latch on to anything available, anything that will provide some support, stability, comfort, joy or happiness. Now, when you change the software with the five disciplines of vana-prastha, then the coverings drop one by one. When all the coverings drop, luminosity of mind is experienced, effulgence of mind is experienced. That mind is a sattwic mind; it is a spiritual mind.

The revelations of Ezekiel in the Bible describes the mystic visions that Ezekiel has. He sees seven curtains and light behind them. As each curtain is being removed, the light becomes brighter and brighter. At the end he has the vision of pure luminosity, light. Sri Swamiji has spoken about it in kundalini yoga. He says that the chakras are the layers which block the luminosity of pure consciousness from expressing and manifesting. As the effects or dimension of each chakra

is transcended, the mind becomes purer and purer. There is more radiance, more luminosity, more knowledge, more wisdom, more awareness, more creativity. What has been spoken of in the Bible is the subject of kundalini yoga. The seven curtains are the seven chakras. This is not a new idea; rather, it is an idea that has been defined by various cultures and traditions over the ages. All the spiritual traditions speak of the luminosity of the self and how it is possible to access it.

To access the self, the dross of the mind has to be removed. That becomes the lifelong effort, sadhana, of the spiritual aspirant. In yoga, every act that you perform, every thought that you think should lead you to lessening the grossness of the mind. Only then can one be called a yogi, a practitioner of yoga. Otherwise you will be a gymnast. Most yoga practitioners are like gymnasts. They stand in front of a full-length body mirror to see how well they are doing the posture. A real yogi is not one who practises asana and pranayama, but one who explores the nature, changes the patterns of the mind and cultivates proximity to spirit, which is known as *atmabhava*.

Atmabhava or paramartha bhava is the main projection of the mind in the third and fourth stages of life, while the self-oriented bhava, *swartha bhava*, or sentiments limited to oneself, are the main projections of the mind in the first two stages of life. Sri Swamiji has spoken about cultivation of atmabhava as the aim of yoga and spirituality: coming closer to the nature of the spirit, coming closer to the nature of luminosity.

When there is atmabhava, there is an increase in inner sensitivity. You are able to understand the cause of suffering. Right now you are only undergoing suffering, but when there is atmabhava one understands the cause of suffering. Right now you only know that you are suffering and that you want to be free of it, and you pray to God to free you, but you do not understand the cause of suffering. With the experience of atmabhava, the potential of the mind

48

expands, for the veils of maya are removed one by one. The mind which was tamasic is now becoming suffused with sattwic qualities. The mind in which negative qualities predominated is slowly becoming free of these and is cultivating positive qualities. The mind which was selfish is now becoming selfless. It is able to see everyone just as it used to see only itself. It experiences oneness with all. Thus, the attainment of atmabhava is the result of the education of vanaprastha, which is able to transform the nature, samskaras, behaviour and actions of the mind.

Once you have had the glimpse of atmabhava, then your journey into sannyasa begins. Real sannyasa, real dedication, understanding and creativity manifest when you have atmabhava, proximity to your spirit. Sri Swamiji has said many times in his satsangs that this should be the purpose and goal of every aspirant. He also says, "As long as I was exploring different methods and means to discover myself, I had to struggle. But when I cultivated atmabhava, my path became clear." This was his sentiment. The path becomes clear when one cultivates atmabhava. The first software becomes redundant and the second software replaces the first one.

Sannyasa ashrama: fullness of giving

The fourth ashrama, *sannyasa*, does not mean renunciation, but pooling together the resources that one has, to help others. That is the meaning of the word sannyasa. *Sam* means totality, and *nyasa* is trust. Just as in society a legal trust is created to fulfil an objective, in the same manner, in sannyasa one pools together all one's resources, strengths, creativity and potential into a trust, in the nyasa, whose purpose is to help and uplift others.

The system of discipline is nyasa. It is with nyasa that lifestyle modification begins, even in the stage of a learner or bramachari, the stage of social responsibilities or grihastha, or the stages where one is an adherent of dharma and moksha: vanaprastha and sannyasa. This discipline is necessary and nyasa happens at each level of these four ashramas.

49

It is only at the end that it becomes *sam* or absolute, total. Therefore, one begins to cultivate one's nyasa, one's attitude, awareness, consciousness, perception and aspiration right from studentship.

Nyasa takes a new form when you take up social responsibilities, it takes another form when you retire from life, and nyasa takes another form when you commit yourself to do some good for humanity. When you commit yourself to do some good for humanity, then that nyasa is known as sannyasa. Shankaracharya, who was the re-organizer of the tradition and advocated the Advaita Vedanta philosophy, said that without discipline and without re-educating oneself, it is not possible to progress in spiritual life. Therefore, after one has completed the steps of vanaprastha one moves into the sam-nyasa area.

When, by practising swadhyaya, satsang, sadhana, seva and sanyam, one is able to bring about a transformation in life, the natural consequence is that all one's energies and abilities are utilized for the welfare of others. A person whose entire energy is involved in the welfare of others is a sannyasin. Wearing the colour geru does not qualify one as a sannyasin, though that is also necessary, as it provides strength to the tradition and makes one's goal clear, but the essential factor is manifestation of the selfless quality in life, changing the selfish vritti to a selfless vritti.

When one follows the sequential path and arrives at sannyasa ashrama, the desire to help others becomes so intense that one forgets oneself completely. Thus, in the first two ashramas one works for oneself and in the next two ashramas one works for others, one's actions are oriented towards dharma and moksha.

Moksha does not mean God-realization; it means freedom from the lacks of life, it means fulfilment. If there is sorrow, then freedom from sorrow is moksha; if there is deprivation, then fullness is moksha. Thus, moksha is poornata, wholeness, and wholeness is behavioural, mental, emotional and spiritual.

Misinterpretation of the ashrama system

There is one point that must be clarified. People who are immersed in the pleasures and passions of the senses try to find all kinds of ways and means to remain there. They try to justify their actions and thus say, "Make the effort towards dharma and moksha only when half your life is over." People possess bartering minds; therefore, they say that if the human lifespan is presumed to be a hundred years, divide it equally among the ashramas: spend twenty-five years in brahmacharya ashrama, twenty-five in grihastha, twenty-five in vanaprastha and twenty-five in sannyasa. But the question that arises is: if you opt for vanaprastha or sannyasa in old age, how will you serve society? Instead, you will want to be served by society. The tradition says that whenever you experience the inclination and intensity, you may change your lifestyle. The day there is an intense desire to transform oneself, it is time to walk a new path of life.

If one had to follow the twenty-five-year rule, then there would not have been a Shankaracharya, Vivekananda, Sivananda or Satyananda. A person who has come into this world with certain samskaras from past births, whose destiny is to walk this path, will not be bound by social injunctions. His destiny was written out by Providence. Did our sages not know that a higher will writes the destiny of every individual, not man and not society? Our ancestors knew this very well and they also knew that there are *yogabhrashtas*, those who did not complete their spiritual journey in the last birth. Some part of the journey is still left, so they have to take birth again. Thus, when the concept of yogabhrashta exists in our culture, when our scriptures and sages have spoken of the writ of destiny, when they have spoken of past samskaras and karmas, will they say that you follow the systems of society instead of your destiny? No.

Remember these words, for I am clarifying the thoughts of the sages. The ashrama system is not a rigid system. Our sages recognized that the mind is affected by the samskaras and qualities that one is born with and that they will be expressed. Sri Swamiji used to attain the state of samadhi at the age of six. A person who manifests such samskaras has a destiny to fulfil, and which individual, family, society or social system can stop him? Which social system could stop Ramana Maharshi or Swami Sivananda? Read the life story of any saint or sannyasin of India and you will find that they could not be held back by any social system or family, for there was intensity in their samskaras, karmas and destiny. Nevertheless, it remains true that you need to fulfil all the duties and purpose of whichever ashrama you are in, and then move on to the next. And it is you who must decide when your obligations to a particular ashrama have finished.

4

Ashtanga Yoga of Sannyasa
The eightfold path of transcendence

In order to change the software of the mind from a material programming to a more luminous, balanced, harmonious, integrated and spiritual programming, you have to subject yourself to the eightfold path of transcendence or the eightfold path of sannyasa. Just as in order to experience meditation, samadhi or awaken the kundalini one has to go through a series of yoga practices or techniques, in the same way, in order to cultivate spiritual awareness, one has to go through a series of learnings.

This series of learnings has eight stages. The first five belong to the vanaprastha ashrama where one is exploring oneself, and the last three belong to sannyasa ashrama where one is committing and dedicating oneself to a higher purpose and realigning with the will of God. The first five are swadhyaya, satsang, seva, sadhana and sanyam, and the last three are viveka, vairagya and samarpan. These constitute the ashtanga yoga of a sannyasin. Just as there is the ashtanga yoga of Patanjali, constituting yama, niyama, asana, pranayama, pratyahara, dharana, dhyana and samadhi, for a sannyasin the ashtanga yoga consists of swadhyaya, satsang, seva, sadhana, sanyam, viveka, vairagya and samarpan.

FIVE INITIAL STEPS IN VANAPRASTHA

1. Swadhyaya: foundation of transformation

The foundation of change and developing a different lifestyle is built with swadhyaya. *Swadhyaya* is often translated as 'self-study'. It is a process by which you can know yourself and realize, know your mind, emotions, nature, character and personality. This is the beginning of swadhyaya. There are many different levels of swadhyaya, of self-observation. The first is study of oneself and the second is study of literatures which can more precisely deepen understanding and knowledge.

In the first level you analyze yourself, and come to know your shortcomings and weaknesses, qualities and strengths. You analyze yourself and try to bring about a balance in the extreme expressions of your nature and personality. Swadhyaya is not picking up a book and memorizing it, but implementing and adopting what you know in your life. Once you know your strengths and weaknesses, you can balance them out and use your capabilities for a good cause. You can do something useful for society, inspire others and help them arrive at the right way of thinking. This is known as living according to dharma. This is what brings about peace, prosperity and happiness. When there is an absence of dharma there is anarchy, suffering, struggle, hatred and conflict. All these things exist inside the mind, not outside. It is the mind which connects with desires or with dharma. Therefore, the first change in mental direction is brought about with swadhyaya. Try to know yourself, try to understand your desires, the qualities you are trying to imbibe and the attainments you are aiming at. Thus, in the first level of self-observation the SWAN principle needs to be applied: analysis of your strengths, weaknesses, ambitions and needs.

Usually people identify with their weaknesses and inabilities and ignore their capacities, strengths and qualities. They begin to cry and curse saying, "I am weak, I am not able to do this, I am incompetent." You develop a peculiar self-image when you identify with your weaknesses and shortcomings.

54

However, if you begin to analyze and identify with your strengths, then the mind opens up. The possibilities inherent in the mind begin to flower, for positivity is compost for the mind.

Negativity is poison for the mind. This is true and don't take it lightly. Those who think negatively, critically and are pessimistic, are not capable of keeping in sight the beauty and the good that life has offered to them. They are only looking at the bad and the ugly, which is emanating from their own mind. Life has given everyone the same opportunities, but the pessimistic attitude is a projection of the mind, representing a tamasic mind. That negative attitude and condition of mind is poison. You don't see the happiness, joy or beauty anywhere. If you observed the beauty and opportunities that life has given to you to evolve and develop, you would be happy and grateful.

55

No matter what kind of a day you've had, difficult or easy, at night look at what you learnt that day, and thank guru and God for giving you the opportunity to realize that lesson. It was an opportunity that you received to learn a lesson, to realize a state of mind, to know how to transcend it and be a new person the next day when you wake up. Don't go to sleep thinking about a problem and wake up with the same problem in your mind. Go to sleep thinking about the lesson you learnt during the day with thankfulness in your heart and greater aspiration for a better tomorrow. That is awareness of cultivating the positive components of life.

The more positive you become, the more you are liked by everyone. The more negative and pessimistic you are, the more you are shunned by everyone. That is the reality of life. So, make a choice: identify with your weaknesses and shortcomings and cry all your life, or identify with something beautiful which can motivate, guide and inspire you to tread a new path. This understanding has to come from applying the SWAN principle. Know your strengths, weaknesses, ambitions and needs. Identify with the strengths, fulfil your needs, prioritize your ambitions and accept your weaknesses. This is the beginning of swadhyaya, and the practical way to change the mental software.

The mental software is the karma with which you have come into this life. When you buy a computer it comes with a basic operating system. Then, according to your choice and need, you can fit in different softwares, using the same basic operating system. In your life you have come with a basic operating system called karma, which is the cause of your specific personality. The karmas become the cause of the aspiration for attaining something higher or merely living from moment to moment.

When Sri Swamiji was to be initiated into sannyasa, he asked Swami Sivananda, "What do I do after sannyasa?" Swami Sivananda replied, "The same as you have been doing all this time, no change in lifestyle. The same seva, the same departments, the same routine, nothing changes. However, there is a difference. After you have taken sannyasa, your purpose should not be to accumulate karmas in your life, not to bind yourself to the world, but to free yourself from karmas and the world. Therefore, when you perform an action, think that you are not performing it for yourself, but offering it to guru. This will make you free from the results and effects of the actions you perform. Over a period of time, you will be able to exhaust your karmas, your aspirations, desires, ambitions and motivations. When you have exhausted your karmas, then embark upon a new life."

Swami Sivananda used the phrase 'exhaustion of karma'. What is this exhaustion of karma? It is changing the operating system. However, this change will come about with swadhyaya, which begins with the discovery of your own nature and character, and that is the first stage.

The second stage of swadhyaya is the input of wisdom in the mind. In the novice stage, the brahmachari stage, there was input of information and knowledge in the mind. You studied history, geography and maths. You sat exams and passed them to move on to the next class. In the same manner, you need to read, imbibe and understand the literatures, the scriptures in which spiritual life is elucidated. By reading them, you begin to understand yourself from a different perspective. The understanding may not be perfect, but a beginning is made. What is begun starts to mould your thoughts, ideas and concepts, and give you a different perspective and vision.

Thus swadhyaya has to be seen in two main categories: the study of one's own character, nature and personality, and the study of literatures and scriptures by which one can strengthen spiritual understanding and awareness. When you study the spiritual sciences and continue self-study at the same time, you are able to live what you read. You watch how you live and acknowledge what the sages have prescribed. Thus what you know and what you do become one. That is the first component of sannyasa yoga.

2. Satsang: input of positivity

The second step is *satsang*: discussion, communication, positive and creative inputs into the mind, for better and positive thoughts, behaviour and actions to generate. Most of the time people indulge in criticism and negative talk: "This person is like that, that person is like this, I don't like that person, I like this person . . ." This is negative talk, critical talk, me vs you. Gossip and criticism are negative injections for the mind, whereas positivity and creativity are positive injections for the mind.

Satsang gives you the opportunity to discriminate between the right injection and the wrong injection. If you take the right injection on time, you can avoid many illnesses. If you take your B-complex injection once a year, you can avoid many physical problems. Similarly, if you give the right injection to your mind, the right thought, you will be able to avoid many problems in relationships, behaviour, attitude and health, and be the winner.

The literal meaning of *satsang* is company of the good and the virtuous, company of truth. It does not mean a lecture. However, to provide a broader perspective on the meaning of satsang the *Ramacharitamanas* says: *Prathama bhagati santan kara sangaa* – "The first step in bhakti is company of the pious."

Sant means a good person and *asant* means a bad person. If we are surrounded by negative people it will not be called a satsang environment, for our mentality will become like theirs. However, if we are surrounded by good people, goodness will enter our minds. Therefore, watch your environment and recognize who you are with. A positive person is one who provides inspiration, enthusiasm and joy. You have to increase your association with such people and stay away from those who complain and criticize. In this way, create a good environment for yourself. This is one definition of satsang.

The second definition is being infused with good thoughts. When you listen to a spiritual talk, for instance, it

58

is possible that you will remember one sentence which struck you. It is not possible to remember the entire talk, but the one sentence that struck you may start off a new train of thought in your mind. It will start off a new search. Therefore, try to imbibe positive thoughts. Read good things, speak good things, hear good things and see good things. Thus, the first meaning of satsang relates to one's company and the second to thoughts.

Satsang is positive and constructive communication. This positive injection for the mind provides inspiration and ideas so that what you did not understand or know becomes clear, and different centres of learning open up in the brain. The mind becomes stronger and resolute; it receives a direction so you can free your self from the illusions of the world, and this is the second step to change the mental program.

3. Seva: practising non-doership
The third component is seva, service. Service is nothing but action. Service is a word which indicates that you are engaged. What you are engaged in is an activity or some active event.

Seva is twofold, self-oriented and selfless. When actions are performed with personal motivation, for the fulfilment of a personal need, expectation or desire, they are known as self-oriented, self-gratifying or selfish actions. They are meant to satisfy the person who is performing them. The term 'selfish action' is not used in a negative sense here, but indicates that self-oriented behaviour and desire is predominant in those actions. The other form of action is selfless, when there is no personal desire or expectation, only performance.

All the scriptures say that as long as you have social responsibilities, you are selfish. Whatever you do at this time is for your own stability, gratification, fulfilment and enjoyment. However, traits of selflessness are seen from time to time in your life even when you are predominantly selfish. When your actions begin to help others and are not performed for your gratification or pleasure, they become selfless actions. Seva implies action which can be selfish or selfless, though commonly it is identified more with selfless action.

Performing selfless action is difficult. Only a person whose mind is clear can put a plan into force for performing selfless service. You want to perform selfless service, but don't know how. You begin to think that treating the sick and serving the old is selfless service, but that is not the real concept of selflessness.

Selflessness means to come out of your own shell. Your mind which was identifying with yourself has to identify with others. You have to perceive the world not as a stranger, but as part and parcel of your own life expression. When you feel that everyone is part and parcel of your own life, then selflessness begins. Selflessness will manifest if you begin to feel that each person is part of your life.

After all, when you look after your children, knowing and believing that they are part of your life, some of your actions towards them are selfless and some are self-oriented. Both self-oriented and selfless actions are the same. In the professional arena also, streaks of a selfish and a selfless approach are both seen. However, it is difficult to be totally selfless when living as a householder in society. So, there has to be a process of learning how to become selfless, and the teacher is the guru. Thus in India it is said that to learn the real meaning of seva, go to a guru ashram.

Seva cannot be learnt as an external action. In order to perfect seva, go to a guru and serve him or her. The guru will teach you that whatever you are doing is not for yourself; it is as an offering to God. That basic instruction is learnt from the guru. You have read about it, but not practised it. Only when the guru tells you will you begin to do it, not before that, no matter how many books you read. This will happen if there is faith and trust in the guru. If there is no faith and trust, then the guru is not guru for you, only a wise person. If there is faith and trust, then guru and disciple are like two windows in the same room that open to allow the air of selflessness to blow through.

Sri Swamiji tells of an incident with his guru in Rishikesh. Swami Sivananda had given instructions that ashram inmates had to properly serve the sick people who came to the ashram. The sick were treated at the ashram and upon recovery, Swami Sivananda would send them off with clothes, grains and money. Once, Swami Satyananda and Swami Chidananda brought a leper to the ashram. Swami Sivananda saw the sick man and instructed the two disciples to 'serve the Narayana' – Swami Sivananda always referred to all as 'Narayana'.

This man was in a bad shape and had innumerable wounds with pus oozing out of them. Every day Swami Satyananda and Swami Chidananda would clean his wounds and look after all his needs. One day, as Sri Swamiji was dressing his wounds, he happened to press a bit too hard. The man screamed and slapped his face. Sri Swamiji was young and hot-blooded and became furious. He went to Swami Sivananda and said, "Get someone else to serve your Narayana! He slapped me. I am not going back to him." Swami Sivananda smiled and said, "This is Narayana testing your commitment to seva", and sent Sri Swamiji back to the man.

Even in seva one may experience reaction. Whatever work one does can bring forth a reaction, whether it be selfish or selfless. There is always an expectation from one's actions; therefore, there is reaction. Even if the guru is standing before you asking you to do something while another person there continues to abuse you, for how long will you be able to endure the abuse? All these reactions are due to the ego and they are managed with seva. The ego is reduced through seva and you are able to control your behaviour.

Ego management is only possible through selfless seva, not self-oriented seva. Self-oriented seva will enhance the ego while selfless seva will reduce the ego. Seva is the third step for changing the software.

4. Sadhana: sustained effort

The fourth aspect is sadhana. *Sadhana* means practice and it has to be done in a sustained, continuous manner, with the conviction that it will lead you to your goal. It has been said:

Sa tu deerghakaala nairantaryasatkaaraasevito dridhab-hoomih. (YS 1:14)

It (practice) becomes firmly grounded by being continued for a long time with reverence, without interruption.

Sadhana is the effort which you make for a long time, *deerghakaala*; which you do continuously, *nairantarya*, and in which you have faith, *satkaara*, that it will lead you to fulfilment of the destined desire. Therefore, condition your mind for sadhana.

People don't understand what sadhana is. Sadhana is not something that you decide on a whim. It is not sitting for eight hours to meditate. When people get the urge to practise sadhana they want to meditate for many hours straight and receive instant benefits. They don't understand that if they practise meditation for one minute a day for eight years, they are more likely to attain the desired goal. If you practise for eight hours on one day, it will not be beneficial, for you are

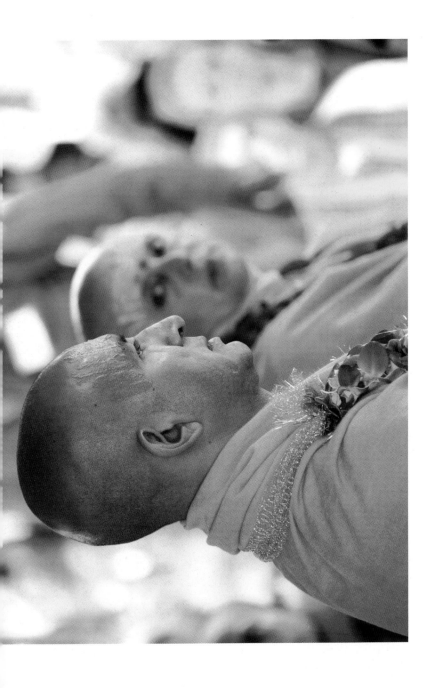

not conditioned to it. You don't know how to swim and you have jumped in at the deep end.

Sadhana has to be developed. Start with one minute of stilling the mind, then increase it to two minutes, then three minutes, then four minutes, then five minutes. Increase the moment of stilling the mind minute by minute. This conditions the mind and it is called sadhana. If you try to sit for half an hour trying to still the mind, you will be a failure, as you are trying to prolong the sadhana period beyond your natural ability and inclination. Why do you want to prolong the sadhana period? Why do you want to meditate for one hour a day, when the same benefit can be had in five minutes? Do you think that by meditating more, the progress will be rapid?

If you have a headache and you take one aspirin, your headache goes away in ten minutes. Will your headache go away in one minute by taking ten aspirins? Even if you take ten aspirins, it will take ten minutes, and the extra nine will damage your system. Sadhana has to be looked at in the same manner. If the natural progression and growth of the

mind will take ten years by practising one minute daily, fine. At least you will be able to adjust and accommodate to the change within. When you cannot adjust and accommodate to the changes within, a crisis takes place, and those who meditate for long go through mental crises.

One day a family came to me, and the husband said, "Swamiji, my wife is losing all interest in society. When people invite us, I want to go but she says, 'No I will not go.' How far can we avoid our friends and family?" I asked her, "Why do you do that?" She said, "Swamiji, I have developed a very intense vairagya." I said, "How come?" She said, "I meditate for hours every day." I said, "You are not developing vairagya, you are developing a crisis in your life. You are experiencing aloofness and isolation from everything, and you are not aware of the social responsibilities that you have to fulfil. Please don't meditate, and if you meditate then don't come to me. My instruction and order is: don't meditate, and if you do want to meditate, make it only ten minutes a day."

She did not disobey, but there are many who would. They would say, "What ten minutes! I can sit for half an hour, my legs will cooperate." You are more aware of your legs than your mind! You say, "My legs will allow me to sit in meditation for half an hour, therefore I will sit for half an hour," but you don't consider your head or mind. Besides, what do you meditate on? Light? If you want to see the light, turn on the switch and you can see light with your eyes open. Have you ever experienced the light that you want to see? No, because there are too many vasanas, samskaras, aspirations, expectations and desires. Your mind is like an onion. Remove one layer, another is there, and another, and so on. All these layers have to be removed before you can know the real nature of the mind. Yoga is clear on this subject.

Sadhana means that you do something continuously, without any break or obstruction until you have perfected it. I will give you an example from my early ashram life of a sadhana

64

I did when I was young to change a behaviour of my mind. I was always defeated by one instinct: sleep. It used to be a big problem. I could sleep for sixteen hours! Sleep was one vritti that defeated me earlier. The problem was that when I was asleep my guru brothers would put the cot outside the ashram gates. I would find myself waking up with the full sun shining on my face and strangers on the road looking down at me.

I asked my guru brothers how they woke up early and they said, "We use alarm clocks." I observed the people who had alarm clocks. They would wake up at four in the morning and keep on yawning the whole day long. I thought, "What is the use of waking up so early if you are going to be sleepy all day!" One swami was a expert in that. He used to wake up at four o'clock to the morning alarm, then after breakfast at six o'clock he would disappear. He would appear again and after lunch disappear, then he would appear again and after dinner disappear. He would sleep under his chowkie during the day, so when people searched for him, he would not be found in his room. When I observed that I thought, "What is the use of waking up at four and then trying to find moments to sleep during the day! What should I do?"

I found a solution. I said to myself, "If I am waking up at eight o'clock, I will set my alarm for 7.55 for one week, 7.50 the next week, 7.45 the week after," and gradually five minutes by five minutes I trained my mind, and it was easy. To manage five minutes less sleep for a week was simple. It conditioned my nature and eventually four o'clock was no problem. If I had used the alarm, then the whole day I would be yawning, as it would be a forceful effort. Such forceful effort does not change the quality, nature or behaviour of the mind. However, a gentle movement of the mind towards the desired direction can alter its nature and behaviour. That is the meaning of sadhana: little by little you bring about a change in the normal pattern of living, a change which is permanent.

5. Sanyam: restraining the behaviour

The fifth component of changing the software is *sanyam*, restraint, and restraint means learning the discipline of appropriateness. It means observance of rules. Not the rules which are written down on a notice board, but those which connect you with appropriateness, rules that you know inherently. All of us know how we should behave where and before whom. One who observes the rules, practises appropriateness and does not cross the boundaries is called *sanyami*. Such a person is able to keep the senses under control and not allow them to become engrossed in enjoyment. Instead, the person becomes a witness of the enjoyment and the desire for it. Understanding the need for

enjoyment, he chooses to either go towards it or away from it. The basis of sanyam is, therefore, knowledge of objects, of their usefulness and necessity, and knowledge of one's own greed and desires. With the help of this knowledge, one keeps one's mind under control, keeps the sense attractions under control. When there is sanyam, one still does everything, but not obsessively.

By cultivating sanyam one is also able to handle any kind of behaviour. For instance, when you have retired from professional life, people may not accept your authority any more. At that time, if there is sanyam, one will not feel the need to order people about for it is no longer appropriate to do so, but will continue to hold one's inner balance.

Generally people think of discipline as restriction. They say, "This or that place has very hard discipline." You feel that because you are not aware of the effect such discipline can have on you. I have lived a disciplined life, I have lived in a disciplined environment, I have lived with Sri Swamiji. Those disciplines were not restrictions, but they allowed a better nature to manifest.

Many people find it difficult to follow mouna in the ashram. If you can't keep quiet for an hour or half an hour during a meal, then what do you expect of yourself? If you cannot stop talking for half an hour while eating, then don't have any high expectations or hopes for yourself. That indicates the frivolousness and fickleness of your mind. With such a mind, you can desire everything like a child, but never understand anything like a mature person. If you cannot regulate the behaviour of the mind, then forget about spiritual awareness or success in material life.

Thus, with these five steps we start the journey in the vanaprastha direction: exploring our nature, building our pool of strengths and qualities, developing our wisdom, generating the creative power within and working to expand the mind. Vanaprastha is an important stage of learning where the spiritual journey begins before you enter into the other level of lifestyle, that of sannyasa.

Sadhana of sannyasa

In the fourth stage of life, sannyasa, the five sadhanas of the third stage continue and a few more are added. Swadhyaya never ends. How do you know that today you can stop self-observation? Satsang never ends. The input of positive inspiration into the mind is an ongoing process. You have to continuously protect your thoughts, your sankalpas, from the negative influences of your own creation or of the environment.

When a farmer sows seeds in the ground, he also makes a scarecrow to shoo away the birds. He makes the necessary effort to protect the seeds that he has sown. He removes the weeds from the site so they don't smother the growth of the small plants. Just as the farmer protects the seeds from being smothered, eaten or destroyed, the good intention of an individual has to be protected. The good aspiration has to be protected and preserved from the negative influences and mentality, whether self-created or stemming from the environment.

Swadhyaya has to continue lifelong, no matter how many changes you make in your life. Satsang is a lifelong process. Seva is a lifelong process. Sadhana is a lifelong process and sanyam is a lifelong process. A few more steps are added when you move to the next stage of life.

THREE REQUIREMENTS OF SANNYASA ASHRAMA

1. Viveka: developing discrimination

Viveka is the discriminative faculty. With the reduction in vasanas, expectations, desires and obsessions, discrimination sets in and you are able to decide whether what you want for yourself will uplift or bind you. If you are able to negate or reject those situations which bind you and accept those which uplift you through your discriminative ability, then that viveka is active. It can guide your actions, behaviour and thoughts in the right direction.

When viveka enters your life, whatever you think is discriminative, for viveka is knowledge and awareness. It is the awareness of right and wrong which you are able to apply in everything. You know whether your thoughts are right or wrong, of a superior quality or a low quality. A discriminative person is not a reactive person. People who react don't have viveka, but people who have the ability to look at a situation twice and think up ways to bring out the creativity from that situation have viveka. If you are able to extract something important and useful even from the most difficult situations, then that is viveka.

Sri Swamiji says, "If I see a person with nine hundred ninety-nine negative qualities and one good quality, I will ignore the nine hundred ninety-nine to extract that one good quality which will overpower all the negative qualities." That is discrimination: knowing that it can be done, that the nine hundred ninety-nine negative qualities will not hamper the emergence of the one positive quality. However, that can happen only if there is proper understanding. When you put yourself through the five sadhanas of vanaprastha, this understanding will invariably come, for all the five sadhanas aim at developing the discriminative power in you, the ability to filter out the illusive from the real. That is the purpose of viveka.

When viveka predominates, the intellect becomes free from all bondages. When the intellect is bound it inclines towards the right or left, there is identification with this or that, and there is no discrimination. However, when there is viveka, the intellect is free of all identifications and can make the appropriate decision. As viveka rises, the discriminative intellect also rises and the bartering intellect comes down. That is when vairagya awakens.

2. Vairagya: transcending attachment

Vairagya is generally translated as detachment. There is a plug and a socket. The plug is in the socket, how do you detach the current from the plug? You can pull out the plug and no current will flow through. That is detachment: removing or separating the point of connection. What is together now is separated. That is how people think of vairagya: cutting yourself off. However, yoga speaks of another way of being detached. Instead of pulling out the plug, just turn off the switch. You can leave the plug connected, nothing will happen. Whenever you want the current, turn the switch on or off. You don't have to go through the exercise of pulling and pushing the plug.

The *Yoga Sutras* say: *Sukhanushayi ragaha* – one is attracted towards those objects which give one pleasure. Therefore, *raga* is attraction for pleasure, fulfilment, happiness and satisfaction. In the state of vairagya, one allows all these things to manifest, but remains free from their influence and craving. You do what you have to, but remain free from the craving. Your association is not with an expectation; it is spontaneous and natural. That is vairagya: living a spontaneous and natural life without attaching yourself, without demanding or expecting anything, but utilizing every resource and situation to uplift yourself. There is no separation, detachment or disconnection, but a developed and better understanding

of how one can use the tools that are available. There is no absence or lack, but the attraction for objects is not there.

For example, children like to eat sweets and force their parents to buy them toffees and chocolates. However, as they grow up they don't feel that uncontrollable urge, though they don't become averse to chocolate. If one has them one will eat them, but one does not feel the need to run to one's parents demanding chocolate. A small change comes about. As you grow older you may walk into a chocolate shop and walk away. There won't be any craving; you can keep the urge under control. This is raga and vairagya. That which you want, desire, crave and cry for represents raga. Thus, vairagya means to first observe the condition which is attaching you to an object and then to slowly remove your mind from it. Viveka and vairagya become one.

Once a mother went to a sage and said, "Please tell my son something. He will listen to you." The sage asked, "What do you want me to say?" She said, "My son eats too many sweets. His teeth are getting spoilt and he is getting worms in his stomach. Please tell him that he should not eat sweets." The sage said, "Okay, come back after a week and I will speak to him." The mother thought the sage would say something very profound. When she returned after a week, the sage said to the boy, "It is not good to eat sweets. Don't eat them." The mother became furious. She said, "Did you call us after a week just to say this? Why couldn't you say it when we came here in the first place?" The sage replied, "Mother, I also had the habit of eating sweets. How could I tell someone else not to do what I myself am not able to stop? So I had to first give up sweets myself. The day I gave them up I could tell your boy that he should not eat them." This is moving from raga to vairagya.

Vairgaya is a state of mental adjustment. You accept that which is, but without feeling attracted to it. Observing it as a witness, you keep yourself free from its attraction. Being a *drashta*, witness, you go on watching the world while remaining established in yourself. One who can watch the world while remaining established in oneself is known as a *vairagi*. Such a one has become free from the feelings of attraction, attachment and the desire for enjoyment. He lives among them, but is free from them. An example of this is an ancient king of India, Maharaja Janaka. He has been called a *videhamukta*, one who is free of the body even while living in it.

Once, Maharshi Vyasa sent his son Shukadeva to Maharaja Janaka to receive teachings on the transitory nature of the world. When Shukadeva reached the royal abode, he noticed that Maharaja Janaka lived in a fabulous palace, sat on a gold throne, wore a gem-studded crown, and appeared like Indra, the king of heaven. Shukadeva wondered how his father could send him to learn about the transience of the world from such a person. How could the world be transitory for a king who lived in such luxury and comfort; the world would be the only truth for him! However, as it was his father's command, Shukadeva went to Maharaja Janaka and said, "Maharaj, my name is Shukadeva. I am the son of Maharshi Vyasa. My father has sent me to you to ask: how can one know that this life is transitory?" Maharaja Janaka said, "Look up." Shukadeva looked upwards and saw that right above the king's throne hung the sharpest of swords, spears and arrows, hanging by a single thread of horse's hair. The king sat under them, aware that any weapon could fall on him at any moment – that he could die at any moment. He said to Shukadeva, "Whenever I sit here, I am aware of only one thing: life is transitory. Therefore, I carry out every duty that I have immediately. I don't leave anything for the next day. Weapons hang in the same way above my bed too. When I go to sleep I don't know if I will be alive the next morning. Therefore, I finish all my work before going to sleep so no one can say I left something incomplete."

Shukadeva prostrated before Maharaja Janaka. Thus, vairagya is where one has everything, yet is free from their attraction, for one understands their transitory nature.

72

When Sri Swamiji used to live in Sivananda Ashram, Rishikesh, he emptied his room completely. He kept a small blanket on the floor, a pillow and a cover, perhaps some paper and a pen because he was the secretary at that time, but nothing more. Swami Sivananda came to his room a few days later and found that there was nothing there, not even a chowkie, forget a stool or chair. He said, "Satyananda, what happened here?" Sri Swamiji said, "I am trying to use the bare minimum of things for myself. I don't require anything else. I have everything that I need." Swami Sivananda did not say anything and went away.

After about half an hour, three swamis arrived with their arms full, carrying tea, sugar, milk, a stove, cups, spoons, saucers, a stool, table, chair and bed. On seeing this, Sri Swamiji said, "What is all this?" The swami replied, "Guruji has sent these for you." Sri Swamiji said, "But I don't need them. Please take them back." The swami said, "Sorry. Orders of guru. We are going to leave everything here, whether you like it or not." Sri Swamiji went to Swami Sivananda and said, "I don't need any things. I am trying to leave behind everything. I am trying to live like a sannyasin." Swami Sivananda said, "Yes, continue to live like a sannyasin. Did you think I sent all that for you? No. I sent them to keep in your room. Not for you." Sri Swamiji said, "But why? I will never use them." Swami Sivananda said, "Who said you were to use them? They are not meant for you. They are meant for those who come to visit you. You hold a post in the ashram. You work during the day and also at night. People come to you in the middle of the night with work. It may be freezing, so give them tea. You don't have to drink it yourself, give it to them. Give the blankets if somebody comes to you at night and feels cold."

In this manner, in the simplest form, Swami Sivananda gave Sri Swamiji the lesson of vairagya. "Have everything, but don't use it for yourself." That is the best lesson in vairagya. Don't be attached. Know the utility of an object and use it properly without thinking that you are its owner or possessor.

Transcend the idea of ownership. Things don't belong to you; they are with you, but they do not belong to you. Don't use them for yourself, but use them when others are in need.

Sri Swamiji carried this teaching of vairagya till the last day of his life. He had everything, but he never used anything for himself. For all the time that he was in Rikhia he did not use a fan, or any other luxury or comfort. He gave instructions to put things in the buildings where guests stay, but not where he stayed and not where sannyasins stay. If people wanted to give air-conditioners for summer, he would refuse, "No. That is not my need." He lived the most simple and natural life, and gave everything that he had to those who needed it.

The spiritual tradition says that vairagya is of three kinds. The highest form is that in which you receive the inspiration to leave behind the excess baggage spontaneously. It is a natural desire to leave behind the excess baggage. Prior to taking that decision, you analyze and understand the requirement of each item in your bag to decide what is necessary and what is unnecessary. Thus the vairagya which comes with such an understanding of appropriateness is the highest form of vairagya. You begin to understand the real nature of things and there are no questions any more. The mentality changes automatically. You don't have to think about it. Things begin to leave you automatically; you don't have to leave anything.

The middle path of vairagya is where you have many questions and are searching for answers, you are searching for something to understand and solve your query. You question: "What is the purpose of this world, what is the purpose of life, who am I?" "What is truth, what is untruth, what is auspicious, what is inauspicious?" In that quest you study different literatures, talk to different people and gradually develop an understanding. When you receive the answers to these questions, you experience vairagya towards the world. After questioning, studying, participating in satsangs, thinking and contemplating, a mental, intellectual and emotional transformation takes place and it makes you turn away from the world. Here, vairagya was not your intention, but by developing an understanding, you arrive at it. It is the result of the enquiry. It is a result of all your queries having been answered.

The lowest type of vairagya is where one is not able to handle the problems of life, everything appears negative, all one's thoughts are negative, and therefore one feels like renouncing the world. It is an infatuation: "I like it, so I have decided to take sannyasa now." Many people come to me with such requests. They wish to receive initiation, but not make any changes in their life. They will go back to the same environment, the same city, house, family, job and tensions and say, "I have become a sannyasin." I am telling you now, that is the lowest form of vairagya, for you are under the influence of an infatuation. Your decision has not been thought about and you don't even know if you qualify. You have not trained yourself, so how you can take sannyasa? First train yourself for twelve years under the guidance of a guru and then think of poorna sannyasa. The sudden impulsive decision is the lowest form of vairagya. In fact, a sannyasin is one in whose life things leave by themselves, and the world ceases to have any attraction.

3. Samarpan: flowing in surrender

When one understands the transitory nature of life and the world, *samarpan*, surrender, follows naturally. Until then one remains rigid. When the transience of life is understood, one surrenders oneself.

There is an incident related in the *Mahabharata*. Once, a *yaksha*, manifestation of the higher force as spirit, quizzed Yudhishthira, and the first question was, "What is the biggest surprise in the world?" Yudhishthira replied, "Every day people are born and die. Everyone knows that they will die one day, yet no one wants to die. This is the biggest surprise of the world." Despite knowing we must die, we want to keep death at bay. However, when one is able to accept death, when one is able to accept the transience of life, one connects with the everlasting truth. One surrenders to the higher force. Therefore, as vairagya becomes intense, surrender takes place naturally.

The idea of surrender is: 'Let thy will be done'. Nothing more than that. With vairagya, one dies to the world, one is no longer infatuated by the pains and pleasures of the world, and one gives oneself over to God, one automatically moves into the surrendered mentality. With the intensification of vairagya, the thought 'Thy will be done' becomes stronger. One continuously lives the thought: 'All is yours, nothing is mine.' At that time, one cultivates a special qualitative relationship with the inner self or *atma*, and with the higher self, *paramatma*. That is sannyasa.

The initial five steps in the eightfold path of transcendence – swadhyaya, satsang, seva, sadhana and sanyam – indicate a quality, a determination, an effort in which you are trying to make your mind harmonious and pure. It is the purity which counts, not the hours of meditation – purity of intention, thought, mind, energy and expression. As you elevate yourself more and more, you become purer. So the five initial stages bring about purity in thought, speech, action and behaviour. They bring in understanding, open your mind to new experiences, and then it is given a direction. This new state of mind which you acquire through the five initial sadhanas is given a direction to focus on in sannyasa life. The direction to focus on is samarpan.

To walk towards samarpan, total and absolute surrender, you need the crutches and support of the previous two aspects, viveka and vairagya. Without viveka and vairagya, surrender is not possible; whatever you think will only be an intellectual surrender.

Aim of sannyasa: improvement, not realization

To perfect sannyasa one has to follow all the eight stages. They are essential to transform the mind and bring it to a state of calm where it has been removed from the objects of pleasure and become established in itself. The *Yoga Sutras* describe this process as: *Yogah chitta vrittih nirodhah*. Stop the dispersed flow of the vrittis of the mind and bring them to a unidirectional flow. The result will be: *Tada drashtu swaroope avasthanam*, experience of inner stillness.

Just as one needs a scrubber to clean utensils, one needs the eight steps to clean the mind, to elevate its materialistic state from earth and connect it with the spiritual realm. That is the effort for dharma and moksha. The effort for dharma begins with the first five steps of swadhyaya, satsang, seva, sadhana and sanyam. They free one from the material conditioning. One is able to gather one's dispersed thoughts, become aware of oneself, reduce the negative qualities, enhance the positive qualities and express the appropriate behaviour. The vritti of agitation is renounced and that of peacefulness is adopted. Thereafter, one enters the stage of sannyasa where viveka, vairagya and samarpan play the prominent role.

This series of learnings allows one to become a sannyasin in the real sense of the word. Without these one can never become a sannyasin, no matter how many hours of meditation you practise or how many mantras you chant. In fact, such attempts will only divert the awareness from the actual direction, purpose and focus of sannyasa.

The purpose of sannyasa is not realization. The purpose of sannyasa is to know how one can deal with the expressions and experiences that one undergoes in life, how to improve them and make them constructive. That is what changes the nature and quality of consciousness, making it pure, transcendental and sublime.

Realization is not possible for a human being, only improvement is possible. There is no such thing as realization; there is only improvement of one's nature. You can improve it as much as you like. If you improve by twenty percent, maybe you or others around you will perceive it as a state of realization. I am not denying the word realization; the improved condition of consciousness can be perceived as a realized or awakened state. However, that awakened state is not the final state. You have to keep on going.

You have to keep on improving. This is the concept of spirituality that I understand: make your life positive, optimistic, hopeful and open, express your strengths and qualities, and become better. Expand your mind, expand your consciousness, release your energy. And this is an ongoing process; when it ends, nobody knows. All we know is that it begins when you develop spiritual awareness. How it continues in other dimensions or levels of existence is unknown to us, but in our lives it begins with the awakening of spiritual awareness.

5

Essence of the Path

After going through the process of transformation by following the ashtanga yoga of sannyasa, after awakening and realizing one's own potential, there are certain aspects that have to become part of an integrated life of a sannyasin.

The study

One must study the *Brahma Sutras*, the aphorisms on Brahman or the higher consciousness. Shankaracharya and many others have written commentaries on them. It is a must-study for every sannyasin. The guru then tests the disciple on the study of Brahman, through different methods.

The disciple also has to study the Upanishads and the *Bhagavad Gita*. He has to understand the application of their wisdom. Studying these three – the *Brahma Sutras*, the Upanishads and the *Bhagavad Gita* – is known as *prasthan trayi*. These are the scriptures of a sannyasin.

Sadhana of remembrance

Next is sadhana, sadhana which leads one to *sharanagati*, complete surrender, not partial surrender, but complete surrender, where one is no longer the controller of one's life. To come to this point, the sadhana that helps is mantra, remembrance. Not asana, pranayama, mudra, bandha, shatkarmas, kriya yoga or kundalini yoga. Mantra is the last sadhana of a sannyasin.

79

Sri Swamiji practised all of these and showed us the path. During the panchagni sadhana, he immersed himself in the chanting of mantra. At other times, he always had his sumerini in his hand, moving it constantly – constant remembrance. He said that if he could practise the mantra twenty-four hours of the day, if he could remember the name every moment, then the sadhana would be completed. And he was able to complete it. This remembrance, this mantra sadhana became the rocket for him. He transcended body consciousness, he went beyond the mental dimension; there was no desire, no expectation, nothing to hold him down. In the final stage, the mantra just made him take off. That was when he became *turiyateeta*, free from the effects and bondage of the three gunas.

Living as a bhakta

To come to the point where one is able to surrender oneself completely, one has to become a bhakta. In the *Bhagavad Gita*, Sri Krishna says (12:13):

Adveshta sarva bhootanaam, maitrah karunaa eva cha
Nirmamo nirahankaarah sama dukha sukhah kshami,
(Yo mad bhaktah sa me priyah.)

One who perceives oneness in all, who is friendly and compassionate to all, who is free from attachment and egoism, balanced in pleasure and pain, and forgiving, (such a devotee of mine is dear to me).

Sri Krishna describes a person who is dear to God in the last eight slokas of the twelfth chapter. Only one who is full of the qualities prescribed by God is dear to God, and these are the qualities that a bhakta must possess. Only a devotee who thinks and acts accordingly is dear to God. Sri Krishna has put down the entire list of qualifications of a bhakta and said that anyone who does not possess these attributes is not a bhakta. After all, what kind of a person is able to become a doctor? One who has passed all the medical exams. Similarly, if you are not able to pass even one examination in being a bhakta, you cannot become a bhakta.

Where would you find the kind of person described by Sri Krishna? You are not likely to find such a person in society, in householder life. Perhaps there have been exceptions in history in whom these qualities were seen. However, considering the average mentality of those living the brahmacharya and grihastha ashramas, these qualities are not seen among them, for society and its environment does not support the growth of such qualities.

If someone wants to become *adveshta*, having a unified vision towards all, the first people to oppose them would be their parents. They would say, "What are you doing? You are ruining the home. You are distributing all your earnings to others." This has happened in the life of many a saint. Inspired by compassion they would give away all the household goods to the needy. That mentality does not exist among average

householders, and the material mentality which they possess does not support the growth of the qualities of devotion.

To become adveshta one needs to remove all the feelings of *dveshta*, fragmented vision, and it is a lengthy and arduous effort. How does one become free from the feeling of *dwaita*, duality? How does one become free from the feeling of you and I, big and small, superior and inferior? One can spend an entire lifetime trying to become adveshta. One can spend a whole lifetime trying to acquire *maitri*, friendliness, and *karuna*, compassion. One has to put in the effort again and again; these qualities are not achieved in a single stroke. In fact, only those who come into this world to perform a divine task are equipped with the samskaras that manifest these qualities. Thus, it is believed in our tradition that a sannyasin is endowed with special talents, for he is able to join the flow of his mind with God or the guru tattwa.

Understanding the relationship with God

In a sannyasin's life, surrender receives an aim, a focus, a connection between you and your guru, between you and your God.

God for a sannyasin is *nirakara*, unmanifest. A sannyasin does not adhere to a particular philosophy or belief. He can represent everything and be above everything. There is openness, acceptance and understanding of the essence of the tradition. Sannyasins do not belong to any one religion or belief, but can represent every religion and belief.

The personal direction of a sannyasin exists in the theory of monism, which states that there is no duality in the world; we are all part of the same spirit. The same spirit shines in each one of us; there is no difference. That is the ultimate attainment, where God is realized in the world and the world is seen in God – where infinity can be seen in a grain of sand.

Necessity of guru

The guru and his teachings provide the opportunity for the qualities and realization of sannyasa to blossom in a disciple's life. That is the purpose of a guru's teachings. The purpose is not to provide you with moksha; rather, one attains moksha as a result of following the teachings. Hunger is automatically satiated when you eat, but in order to eat you need to make the effort to procure food, you need to make the effort to satiate your hunger. Similarly, to receive the learning of sannyasa, you have to be in the proximity of guru. It is not possible to achieve it on your own, for you are not the controller of your mind.

You have to use the mind to change its own nature. Do you know your own defects? Do you know your own responses and reactions? Do you know your own strengths? Do you know your own limitations? Therefore, the learning has to take place not at home in society, but at the ashram in the presence of guru, not by reading books on samarpan, seva, sadhana and sanyam, or adopting any of them while fulfilling your responsibilities towards family and friends. That is not the learning of sannyasa. The mind is not being guided; it is only your inquisitiveness and curiosity which makes you question, "Shall I do this, shall I do that?" There is no adherence to an instruction or guideline. Therefore, the education of sannyasa can take place only in an ashram in the presence of a master.

The connection with guru is most important for a sannyasin. In that connection there has to be clarity and openness, trust and honesty. A sannyasin has to be a mirror that reflects the character and nature of everyone. In order to become such a mirror, the sannyasin must be free from all preconceived notions, thoughts and ideas which create individuality. This art is learned in the proximity of the master, the guru. If there is trust and faith in guru, then guru and disciple become one. Nothing needs to be said. The disciple understands the need of the guru and the guru understands the need of the disciple. This is the highest connection – where two people can live together without expressing any words or thoughts, in absolute unity and harmony.

This connection has to be cultivated and protected over time and this is where many people fail. Most aspirants, sadhakas, fail in this relationship. Nobody has the intention of being a disciple; everybody wants to become something great, a leader, a teacher. However, the beginning of the greatness that you seek is learning to be a disciple. Very few understand this secret.

Initiation is not discipleship. Generally people say, "I have been initiated, I have become a disciple." That is incorrect. With initiation you can become an aspirant, not a member in the social sense, but an aspirant of a spiritual effort. You are making an effort, other people are making an effort, you are all using the same tools to grow, you are all part of the same group – that is initiation. Through initiation you become a *sadhaka*, an aspirant. However, a disciple is a person who is developing a positive, trustworthy, honest, harmonious and open relationship. A disciple is one who follows the disciplines to improve himself.

Remember, discipleship is different from being a spiritual aspirant. Most of you are spiritual aspirants. You can ask yourself whether you are a disciple or not. If you think you are, ask yourself, "What is the percentage of discipleship in me: ten percent, fifteen percent, thirty percent, forty percent, fifty percent, a hundred percent?" You will discover that you are in the 0–50 range. Maybe exceptions go beyond fifty, but the majority will be in the fifty percent range. You are a disciple of the guru and listen to the instructions of the guru fifty percent, and you are a disciple of your own mind and listen to the whims and instructions of your own mind fifty percent. Where convenient you listen to the guru and where convenient you listen to your own mind. How can you say you are a disciple? You are a self-motivated aspirant.

A disciple has no worries about conveniences and inconveniences, as there is a connection and trust that 'my guru will guide me'. A rock does not cry in the hands of the sculptor, but allows the sculptor to chisel away all the excess bits so that the inherent form within the rock may emerge in the form of a beautiful statue. In the same manner, the guru has to be permitted to chip away the excess bits. However, with the first few strokes of the hammer most rocks crack.

Life is full of failures. One example: how many people sustain the practice of their guru mantra every day with

regularity? Very few. So, where is the connection? For food nobody will lag behind, for entertainment nobody will lag behind, even for duty nobody will lag behind. However, in sadhana all aspirants lag behind.

Rethink where you are in sannyasa, rethink what is the percentage of discipleship in you, and you will discover your incompetency and personal clarity.

Protecting the sankalpa

In order to rise above one's failings, the intention has to be protected at all times. Sri Swamiji has said many times that if you have a positive, good and pious intention, you have to protect it from negative influences. Don't allow wild animals to dig up the seed of that beautiful flower of sankalpa which you have planted. Protect it. Find ways to protect it. That is when you can cultivate a relationship with guru. Eventually, the external relationship becomes internal and you discover the source of light inside you which keeps on guiding you, which keeps on inspiring you, which keeps on taking you in the right path in a selfless manner.

6

Dawn of Sannyasa Peeth

Some years ago, after Sri Swamiji had concluded his panchagni sadhana, he gathered all his *kaupins*, loin cloths, made a bundle of them, and gave it to me. Jokingly he said, "Niranjan, if anybody ever asks you what you inherited from Swami Satyananda, tell them proudly that you have inherited his kaupin." He said a very profound thing in a very simple way.

When I was the active head of the yoga movement and president of the Bihar School of Yoga, many people would remark, "Swami Niranjan got an empire on a platter." People used to think that I was the successor of Swami Satyananda's yoga empire, ashrams, centres, resources, disciples, lecturing, teaching, singing . . . The real inheritance was what Sri Swamiji gave me later. He said, "Empires can come and go and administrators can change, but sannyasa is something which is your own for all times to come." That was the significance of his act of giving the kaupins. It meant, "This is my inheritance to you and this is what I want you to become."

When I represented an institution, people offered me the honour worthy of a king and when I became free of the institution, Sri Swamiji gave me his kaupins to indicate that the empire is not my inheritance. The inheritance is the kaupin, which represents a sadhu. It is a symbol of *tyaga*, renunciation. It says: go on renouncing all you possess, keep throwing

off your layers of clothing one by one, and one day you will
be left with nothing but the kaupin. That too will be for the
sake of social propriety, not for you. It says: live without expectations, live your own life and have no expectation from
anyone. That is the learning of sannyasa: live your own life.
That is the path I will be walking now, and it will definitely
be a selective path. Those who want to have the experience
of living that life will have to have a clear mind, whether
they come for one year, three years, five years or ten years.
If you are here for one year, you are here a hundred percent.
No dithering. If you are not here a hundred percent, you

cannot imbibe the teachings of the tradition. What can you imbibe with half a mind? You have to imbibe things with a full mind. If you are here for three years, imbibe with a full mind; if you are here for a lifetime, imbibe with a full mind. Sri Swamiji, our guru, exemplifies one who has lived this tradition.

Fulfilment of sankalpas

Many sankalpas that Sri Swamiji gave before his mahasamadhi have been accomplished. Many promises have been fulfilled, many steps have been taken and more promises and commitments are on the way to fulfilment.

Sri Swamiji had said that it is his wish to see the creation of Annapoorna Kshetram in Rikhia, a place where the children of the Panchayat can be given prasad of one meal a day, not as a government project or social work, but as the prasad of a sannyasin. The work was started during his lifetime and within a year of his mahasamadhi, on the day of Diwali, 5th November 2010, the Annapoorna Kshetram in Rikhiapeeth was inaugurated.

For many people it may not mean anything: a feeding place for children. These thoughts will come to the minds of those who have never suffered the pangs of hunger. You have to understand that although globally we are living in the twenty-first century, India as a nation lives in many different centuries. Some places are in the twenty-first, others are in the twentieth, and still others are in the eighteenth or sixteenth. The facilities, environment and support available are different from region to region. Many people have to toil and struggle very hard to survive. For such people, the basic support – food, shelter and clothing – is important. This support was and is being provided to the people of the Rikhia community as the prasad of Sri Swamiji. No matter how much is accomplished, still there are many people who need such prasad. It is an ongoing work.

There was an occasion during the Sat Chandi Mahayajna in 2009 when Sri Swamiji was sitting in Rikhia. A row of kanyas and batuks was passing before him on their way to the program. Some were laughing, some were talking, some were running, some were walking. Sri Swamiji was watching them with a deep, compassionate gaze. Suddenly he turned towards me and said, "Niranjan, these are children of just one Panchayat. There are thousands of Panchayats like this in India and there are thousands of children there who do not have any future, who will face struggle in life. We are doing this work in just one Panchayat, but in the future it has to be expanded so that the children of this country can have a better future."

Sri Swamiji also said that where a sannyasin or sadhu lives should have the provisions to ensure the children do not go hungry. That sankalpa has been fulfilled. It has been an accomplishment to inaugurate the Annapoorna Kshetram in Rikhia where children can be given prasad of one meal a day. It is the fulfilment of a promise that Sri Swamiji made to the people of the region.

The second promise is the establishment of a proper place for the old, where the elder residents of Rikhia, aged over seventy, will receive the facilities of health care, constructive engagement and a respectable life. This will not be an old age home as in the West, but an expansion and development of the facilities that Sivananda Math already provides to aged pensioners of the village every month.

The third sankalpa and promise which Sri Swamiji made was the establishment or creation of Sannyasa Peeth. That was also accomplished in the year 2010. The formal documents were signed and Sannyasa Peeth was established officially on 6th December 2010, on the first anniversary of Sri Swamiji's mahasamadhi.

There are many miles to go before we rest. 2010 was the year when I rested. It was the first year in my life that I was able to unpack my bags and say Hari Om to my travels, and convey my heartfelt thanks to all those who have supported, aided, sponsored or assisted me in my last twenty-seven years of global yogic wandering.

Three peethas

Our guru has inspired and given direction to three peethas. The word *peetha* means seat, location, place or apex. In 2007, the place that everyone knew as Ganga Darshan Yogashram in Munger was renamed by Sri Swamiji as Ganga Darshan Vishwa Yogapeeth, dedicated to yoga. In the same year, his *taposthali* (place of sadhana) was established as Rikhiapeeth, dedicated to selfless seva. Soon after in 2009, he gave the instructions and guidelines for the establishment of the third peetha, dedicated to sannyasa.

The work of yoga will continue and expand at Ganga Darshan. This is an institution which has been providing yoga training for the last forty-seven years to people of all races, religions, sects and cultures.

When yoga teaching was started in Munger, no one knew about yoga. However, in these forty-seven years, Satyananda Yoga has been accepted all over the world as a pre-eminent system of yoga. The yoga that has been propagated and developed here from the very beginning is a way of life, with the aim of establishing yoga as a world culture.

Yoga is not just an hour-long practice that you do in the morning in the form of asana and pranayama, meditation or japa. People need yoga in their life not only to acquire better health, but also to experience peace and joy. Most people think of yoga as practice, but the result of the practice is a positive and creative change in one's way of thinking, action and behaviour, so one may experience contentment in life. That is where yoga begins; it does not begin with asana and pranayama.

Where is the beginning of education and where is its end? Education begins at kindergarten and ends upon acquiring a degree. In the same way, asana, pranayama, japa and dhyana all constitute the primary class of yoga and a few have entered university. In the forthcoming decade, yoga will be adopted as an inseparable part of life and society.

The essence of yoga needs to be realized and that is when it will become a culture. When there is complete balance in thinking, behaviour, actions and lifestyle, when all that one undertakes is accomplished in a balanced way and there is expression of creativity, then yoga will emerge as a culture, for culture is defined as: *Samyak kritena iti samskritih* – "Harmony in every undertaking is culture."

Thus, the teaching of yoga will continue at Ganga Darshan, and new dimensions of yoga will also be explored and added.

The second peetha, Rikhiapeeth, is where seva is the base, with the aim of upliftment of people with limited resources. The thrust of the work there is to provide basic facilities for the neglected and weaker sections of society. Clothing is provided in abundance, including winter-wear. Housing and education is also provided. Food is provided in two forms: one, enhancement of agricultural facilities so farmers can have a better harvest; two, providing grains to every household as prasad. In this way, the basic facilities are looked after.

Sri Swamiji says that protection to society is not provided by the police or the army. You are safe when you are friendly with your neighbours. If your neighbours are unhappy or

discontented, you are unsafe. Therefore, with seva, fulfil the basic requirements of the neglected section of society. Rikhiapeeth has become the centre of this effort. The work started with one village and now eighty villages receive the prasad of Sivananda Math.

The third peetha is Sannyasa Peeth, for which Sri Swamiji gave instructions in 2009 before taking mahasamadhi. He said to me, "Being free of all responsibilities of the ashram, work in a new direction, for a new purpose and aim. This purpose is revitalization of a spiritual culture for which you have to start a new program. Provide the teaching of kartavya and appropriate living to all in an ashram environment, based on the vedic tradition and culture."

Mandate of Sannyasa Peeth

The commitment thus lies in the formation and development of Sannyasa Peeth. The place chosen for it is Munger, as Sri Swamiji said that Sannyasa Peeth should be established in Munger.

When Sri Swamiji was leaving Ganga Darshan in 1988, we had a talk. He told me, "Niranjan, I am leaving now. I am giving you the responsibility of the yoga movement and yoga propagation. Remember that Ganga Darshan is the accomplishment of a disciple."

I asked him what he meant by 'accomplishment of a disciple'. He said, "When I came to the path of sannyasa, I wanted sannyasa and to live the life that the ancients have prescribed for a sannyasin. However, my guru, Swami Sivananda, gave me a direct instruction. He said, 'Propagate yoga from door to door and shore to shore.' When my guru gave a direct instruction, I set aside all my personal wishes and inclinations, and followed his command. The thought never occurred that I am not able to do what I want to do. If I have committed myself and dedicated my life to my guru, then why think, 'This is my need, my desire, my aspiration'. I have to live as he asks me to live. He gave me a direct order, 'Spread yoga from door to door and shore to shore', which I was able to fulfil from Munger. This place is the accomplishment of the direct order of a guru by his disciple. Therefore, my heart, my soul and my mind will remain in Munger. I may live or travel anywhere, but my dedication and commitment to my guru's mandate is reflected in Munger."

I then realized that Ganga Darshan is not a yoga centre like other yoga centres, studios or ashrams around the world. Ganga Darshan does not come under the category of places where yoga is only a theme. It has a deeper foundation, which is the faith, love, surrender, commitment and dedication that Sri Swamiji had towards his guru. His guru told him, "There will come a time in your life when you will realize that you have fulfilled your obligation to me, that you have freed yourself from the debt to the guru by fulfilling the mandate given to you. When that time comes, you are free to live your life as you have wanted to, as a sannyasin."

Sri Swamiji came to this point in 1983 and handed over the responsibility to me. He spent five more years in Ganga Darshan teaching me the tricks of the trade: how to shine the dark brass and make it sparkle, what kind of agents and chemicals to use to produce the shine. During that period he was mostly in Australia and Europe, but when he felt that my training was complete, he decided to leave. His words have remained with me: Ganga Darshan symbolizes the absolute commitment of a disciple to his guru.

It is not easy to set aside one's own aspirations and thoughts about what one wants to be and do. For all, their own aspirations, whims, desires and thoughts are more important. For Swami Satyananda it was not his whim that took priority, but the mandate of his master. He set aside all his personal aspirations until he was able to accomplish the duty given by his guru. Only after completing what he was told to do, did he leave Munger and start to live the way he wanted to, as a sannyasin. He followed that lifestyle in Rikhia, living in isolation and seclusion, in contemplation and sadhana.

When he said to me, "Now you have to develop Sannyasa Peeth," I took that as an order. Swami Suryaprakash took over the charge of BSY in 2008 and said to me, "Your guru gave you five years. You can also give me five years." I said, "Fine." So, from 2009 when I received the mandate to change my lifestyle, five years will be completed in 2013. I said, "In 2013 we shall celebrate the golden jubilee of Bihar School of Yoga and after that I am free."

Sri Swamiji said, "Continue to live in Munger." I said, "Why? You left. Why should I stay on in Munger?" He said, "I am saying 'Munger', I am not saying 'Ganga Darshan'. Leave Ganga Darshan, but continue to live in Munger and work for the development of Sannyasa Peeth." That was the mandate which he gave to me, and that beginning is being made now.

Role of Sannyasa Peeth

What is Sannyasa Peeth? Is it just another organization, another movement, another building? What will it represent, what will it do?

Of course, this is an evolving subject. So far we have tried to understand the background and theme of sannyasa, and the aspirations of Sannyasa Peeth. Are the sannyasins today adding strength to the tradition or is there something lacking in their learning and sadhana?

The role of Sannyasa Peeth must be seen in the context of our life today, in the context of the direction that human civilization is moving towards. In order to do so, the guidelines have been given in the tradition.

Lifestyle at every stage, from birth to death, is an important factor. How we live, think and act reflects our lifestyle. Somebody once asked a saint, "How can I know you?" The saint replied, "Don't look at the way I eat, dress, walk and talk, but know what I think, how I behave, how I act."

I have learnt this by observing the life of my own guru. I have observed how he lived, what he thought, how he acted and what he was. To know a person, observe their actions, their thoughts, their behaviour, their aspirations, their sankalpa, the determination and drive which they have. Only then can you know a person. However, the majority only see what a person is eating, drinking, who he is talking to and laughing with.

Even as a novice or student, when you are equipping yourself with the tools to survive in the world, if the lifestyle is right, you can cultivate the right strengths, qualities, attitudes, thoughts and mentality to become a learner. When you are in the family, if the lifestyle is appropriate, the entire family can be uplifted. Thus, ultimately, the total human experience comes to lifestyle.

Our ancestors told us the ideal way of life, but people do not walk that path. They have become choosy. They live half a life, the life of a student and a householder. There is the other half of life which only a few have lived, which is called spiritual. 'Spiritual' is only a word, for what is called spiritual

is actually a process of re-educating the mind, the human nature and behaviour. Spirituality brings out the virtuous and positive qualities of life and expresses them. Love, compassion, understanding: these are the positive or sattwic qualities of life. As you develop more and more the sattwic, positive, optimistic and uplifting qualities in life, you become more and more virtuous, you become better, you become good. That state is identified with spiritual life.

Beyond being virtuous, creative and exploring the inner potential, there is no other spiritual life in the human dimension. Thus, according to the precepts, guidelines and instructions of our ancestors, people do not live a full life. They have not yet lived the creative expressions of life. Only a few aspirants try to probe and understand these aspects. They ask: "What is spiritual life, how I can advance in spiritual life, how I can cultivate the spiritual life in me?" This education and understanding, this spiritual wisdom is an important and integrated aspect of human life.

Sannyasa is a form of lifestyle. This lifestyle is all-inclusive. It is learning to live an appropriate lifestyle at every stage of life, including the brahmacharya, grihastha and vanaprastha stages for an understanding of spiritual life to be cultivated naturally. The requisite of sannyasa is selflessness, understanding, intense yearning to know oneself, and many others. You can begin your journey into the qualitative aspect of life by using any of them as your reference point. If you start cultivating understanding, use that as the point to begin your journey. If you practise mantra, use that as the point to begin your journey. If you practise meditation, use that as the point of reference to begin your journey. Whatever you do, use that to begin your journey towards transcendence.

This is the lifestyle that the ancients have spoken about. It is an integrated, holistic lifestyle – bringing about a balance in both the material and spiritual dimensions. You express yourself fully in the material dimension as well as the spiritual dimension.

Sannyasa Peeth will aim at providing an understanding of this lifestyle. It will be a place where one can receive the learning of the duties of life, where one can be equipped with the learning and methods that will be useful for living a complete life. Gradually, it will become a centre where, by understanding the dharma, duties, requirements and attitude needed in every stage of life from brahmacharya to sannyasa, the spiritual and vedic culture will be strengthened.

The essence of the vedic culture has been safeguarded over the ages by the rishis and munis. However, in present times a group of people needs to come forward who have an aim, a dharma and a duty through which the teachings of this culture can be kept alive and imbibed as a way of life. The new generations that are emerging before us are immersed in the attractions of materialism. They are equipped with education, but not samskaras and culture. In Sannyasa Peeth we will provide a new method of life based on samskaras and duty which will be given to young and old alike.

Sage Vyasa says, "O people of the world! I speak the truth – if you follow the path of dharma, you will be able to reach the pinnacle of artha, kama and moksha." What he has said is true. However, to walk this path you need to change your mentality, and look upon all the chapters of life integrally as a way of evolution.

Introducing a lifestyle based on the understanding and application of dharma is the purpose of Sannyasa Peeth. In normal social and family life, one is involved in karma, and there is no rest or gap between one karma and the next. It is a continuous movement from morning to night. When you are involved in the performance of karma continuously, you begin to lose touch and contact with your inner nature. People say, "In the ashram I get the time to do things I can't do at home." That is because in the ashram you are not involved in karmas in the same manner as at home. In the environment that you live in outside, you are driven by your karmic compulsions which don't allow you the freedom to spend the time to discover yourself. You are trying to live your ambitions and that is why you are involved in karma. The more you involve yourself, the more karmas are accumulated. This is the normal pattern of life.

The lives of luminaries such as Swami Sivananda and Swami Satyananda indicate that that they do not live their ambition, they are not involved in karma, but they live their dharma. The awareness and clarity of one's dharma is acquired when there is knowledge of the purpose of life. As long as one does not know what the aim in life is, one is floundering and living karma. However, once one knows the real aspiration in life, the goal and the target, one does not live karma any more; rather, one begins to live one's dharma. This is the shift of consciousness, attitude and mind that is seen in the progression of life, when one begins to live sannyasa life.

Sannyasa is not wearing robes, shaving the head, having a holier than thou attitude or living in isolation or a cloistered environment. That may or may not be a necessary part of sannyasa. People of different mentalities and characters live their lives differently. Some like ashram life and some don't, but the most important thing is cultivation of the right samskaras. Sannyasa is not initiation, sannyasa is not renunciation, but cultivation of the right samskaras so that one may live a life of dharma. Therefore, imparting and instilling of samskaras will be the main function of Sannyasa Peeth.

The learning and sadhana of an integral lifestyle will be taught in Sannyasa Peeth. You may come here to receive certain samskaras, stay for a while, learn the skills of spiritual life and carry that learning back to society. Only those who qualify for sannyasa will be given sannyasa. Sannyasa Peeth does not indicate that everyone who comes there will be initiated into sannyasa or asked to become a sannyasin. Sannyasa Peeth is aimed at bringing about wholeness and completeness in life, to knowing and understanding the sadhanas, thoughts, purpose and aim of all the different stages of life, and as far as possible adopting them in your life. At the end, this is what will bring about evolution and upliftment. You don't need to leave society, but you can leave behind the causes of attachment. You can equip yourself with learning and bring about inner purity.

Sannyasa training in the Satyananda tradition

The first sannyasa training was conducted at Bihar School of Yoga in 1970, when Sri Swamiji himself guided a three-year sannyasa training course. One hundred and eight people came, and out of those, at the end of three years, only eighteen survived. It was a course harder than that of the marines. In actual sannyasa training, the ratio of those who stick it out is only ten percent. It is a difficult training. It involves tapasya, austerity, struggle and hardship to strengthen the mind, to awaken the force, so the understanding may come. Just as a negative thought appears naturally in conflict, understanding should also come naturally in a crisis.

Sri Swamiji used to say, "For sannyasa, I want steel. I want steel which can be put in fire and beaten with a hammer to

give it a shape." These are the words that Sri Swamiji used during the inauguration of the first sannyasa course in which I participated as a nine-year old child. I remember those words even today, "I want steel which can be forged in fire and beaten with a hammer to give it a shape. If you are that steel, come. Otherwise, don't."

Since then, Sri Swamiji's focus was propagation of yoga. He initiated hundreds and thousands into karma sannyasa and poorna sannyasa, but the actual training of the *parampara*, tradition, was given in 1970. Many people have taken initiation and feel that they are part of a yoga family, without understanding what sannyasa is. For many, the dress we wear is a yoga dress; they don't even have the concept of sannyasa. Many others think, "I will wear this dress when I come to the ashram" or "I will wear this dress when I am with my yoga group" – to identify themselves as a member of an organization, but not to identify themselves as a qualified sannyasin of the organization.

Sri Swamiji did not encourage sannyasa training as his focus was propagation of yoga. When he was propagating yoga, he maintained the purity of yoga, whether hatha yoga, raja yoga, karma yoga, kriya yoga, kundalini yoga, mantra yoga, nada yoga or laya yoga. Whatever yoga there was, he maintained its purity as a system, practice, thought, philosophy and lifestyle. Thus, Ganga Darshan is a yoga ashram; it is not a sannyasa ashram. Ganga Darshan represents the yoga component, not the sannyasa component. Although people here try to live the life of a sannyasin, it is not a sannyasa ashram.

Qualifications for sannyasa

Sannyasa Peeth will uphold the highest tradition and not cater to the whims of every individual who wants to adopt geru and then go back to family and society. Sannyasa is not given freely and with the establishment of Sannyasa Peeth, definite restrictions will come. Therefore, do not ask me for sannyasa until you are ready to let go of everything and focus your entire energies and mind on the cultivation of the spiritual qualities in life and their expression.

Sannyasa is a commitment, karma sannyasa is a commitment, jignasu sannyasa is a commitment, even taking *diksha*, initiation, is a commitment. Commitment to what? To improve yourself.

If you are not willing to commit yourself to the lifestyle and disciplines to learn the sannyasa dharma, then sannyasa is not for you. If you are not willing to commit yourself to being a doctor, then don't study medicine. If you study medicine, then have the aspiration to at least become an MBBS, if not a specialist. Whatever profession you opt for, have the commitment to excel in it.

Ask yourself, what have you given to the initiation that you have taken? Today you take mantra, tomorrow jignasu, the day after karma sannyasa and the next day you say, "I am ready for poorna sannyasa." I am giving your own example. It shows there is no commitment; there is only infatuation. You have to refine your lifestyle in order to qualify for sannyasa. However, you can begin the journey from where you are, by following the guidelines as given by the guru, according to your nature, limitations and strengths.

Invitation to Sannyasa Peeth

The work of Sannyasa Peeth begins in 2011, and its first sadhana is a year-long worship of the Cosmic Mother through havan and chanting. This is a personal program to receive the grace, love and compassion of the Mother. We have to first please the Mother for every undertaking and through this sadhana, the ground of Sannyasa Peeth will be created.

As Sannyasa Peeth is an extension of the vision of Swami Sivananda and Swami Satyananda, the period 8th–12th September will become most important for it. September 8th is the birthday of Swami Sivananda and September 12th is the sannyasa initiation day of Swami Satyananda. On these days, starting this year, an annual event will take place at Sannyasa Peeth wherein a special yajna will be performed.

From 2012, we will also start a three-year intensive san-nyasa training course. Over these thirty-six months, every month one topic of yoga will be discussed in depth, both practical and theoretical. It will be a very comprehensive program, which in due course will become the syllabus for Sannyasa Peeth. It will of course evolve and be progressive, but the basic skeleton will be created in the first three-year sannyasa course. This is another plan in the offing.

The official commencement of the activities of Sannyasa Peeth will begin after the World Yoga Convention in 2013. Till then we are preparing, experimenting, working on and finalizing the syllabus, the systems, the methods, the ap-proach. When Sri Swamiji gave me the mandate of sannyasa succession, his intention was that I contribute to the devel-opment of the garden called humanity. In order to make myself capable of doing that, I have to first go through the fire myself. Therefore, beginning from 2010 up to 2013, I am putting myself through the same process that I will be putting the sannyasins through in the future. I am devoting myself to studying the essence of yoga and to thinking how it can be applied practically in life.

Sannyasa Peeth is not going to restrict itself to renunciates or sannyasins only; rather, this institution will provide the right environment, conditions and training – traditional and modern, classical and scientific. Therefore, the whole world is invited to participate in the activities of Sannyasa Peeth.

Everyone's cooperation is necessary for the successful creation of Sannyasa Peeth. You are the ones who will bring about its creation. Contribute in whichever way you can, for this is a work through which the vedic culture will once again become vibrant and society at large will become prosperous. Once all the facilities are in place – accommodation, kitchen, toilets, etc. – then whenever you have the time, come for a month, come for fifteen days, come for three months, come for six months, come for one year. For whatever time you like, come with total focus to experience that life and take some inspiration, some learning, some discipline, and go back and live that. Devote one year of your life to live like a sannyasin, devote two, three, four years, devote whatever time is comfortable and convenient depending on your responsibilities. Sannyasa Peeth will provide an opportunity to live the vedic sannyasa lifestyle for a period of time according to every individual's inclination and commitment to their own development. When people leave after the end of their term, they will go back with the right tools which can be integrated into society. They will be able to live the right samskaras and become a model for their family and friends to live a harmonious life. This will be the teaching of dharma, this will be the teaching of the spiritual sciences in their actual form; this will be the teaching of how one can access the higher consciousness. This is the vision that Sri Swamiji has handed over, and we are embarking on that journey now.

For me, Sri Swamiji is the model of sannyasa. I used his example at the beginning to explain the concept and tradition of sannyasa. I don't have to look at any other scripture,

I don't have to look at any other person. He is the model of my sannyasa. He has been through every stage of life with clarity, conviction, determination and faith. You have only seen him as a guru. For you he is a guru, for me he is a sannyasin. That is the inheritance I have received from him. It is his inspiration, his teaching, his blessing which will develop Sannyasa Peeth. We look forward to this new venture, this new journey.